great songs...

of the pop/rock era

edited by **milton okun**

ISBN 1-57560-602-X

Introduction

Based on the assumption that all listeners are attention challenged, pop music reaches out and grabs you by the ears with a quick intro or riff, quickly lays across a basic story line (often about love lost, won or unrequited), then completes the deal with a painfully catchy chorus, or "hook." Pop music reflects the sounds and rhythms of many different genres, and though it has no musical limitations, time is definitely not on its side: the "classic" pop format averages between two and three minutes in length, total. As a barometer for popular fads and trends, pop music has been the quintessential time capsule. What more would one need to know about the year 1960 after one listening to Chubby Checker's "The Twist"?

The second half of the 20th century produced the greatest crop of popular music composers the world has ever known. As pop music evolved through the 1960s and beyond, the approach to songcrafting—a constant since the turn of the century—underwent numerous changes, resulting in some of the most innovative and memorable moments in music history.

It all began with Bill Haley and His Comets ushering in the modern rock 'n' roll era with 1954's "Rock Around the Clock"; hitmakers like Chuck Berry, Little Richard, and the ever-present Elvis Presley quickly followed. By 1959, record sales had nearly tripled, with most of the action centered around the teen-oriented rock 'n' roll radio market. Though acts like the Everly Brothers ("Cathy's Clown") and Roy Orbison ("Oh, Pretty Woman") penned many of their own hits, many others relied on the songwriting prowess of such professional teams as Jerry Leiber and Mike Stoller, Carole King and Gerry Goffin, and Ellie Greenwich and Jeff Barry. Throughout the early 1960s, the cramped writing rooms inside New York's renowned Brill Building, home to numerous successful collaborations, remained teeming with activity day and night.

It was not to last. As the first major group to write its own hits, the Beatles set a standard in self-sufficiency that was quickly followed by the rest of the pop music world. In New York, Los Angeles, and the other centers of the music industry, the business of pop songwriting—a thriving profession for decades—was dealt a glancing blow. Though the opportunities were far fewer, songcrafting stalwarts like Goffin-King and Greenwich-Barry continued to pump out the hits for the likes of the Monkees, the Animals, and the Righteous Brothers. At Atlantic Records, producer/writer Bert Russell Berns used the same three-chord progression to score a succession of pop classics including the Isley Brothers' "Twist and Shout" and the McCoys' "Hang On Sloopy." Meanwhile, newcomer Jimmy Webb unearthed a string of sophisticated hits that included Glen Campbell entries "Wichita Lineman" and "By the Time I Get to Phoenix."

But by the mid '60s, nearly every important pop group had its own built-in song source—and for a brief period, few could top the Beach Boys' gifted young composer/arranger Brian Wilson. Wilson's crowning achievement came in the form of "Good Vibrations," a three-minute "pocket symphony" that took nearly six months to record at an unprecedented cost of $90,000. A worldwide No. 1 hit, "Good Vibrations" proved that the pop single could be both innovative and commercial; today, it remains a landmark moment in pop history.

More than anything else, pop radio of the '60s and early '70s was a guitar-based medium. Like the Beatles, the Lovin' Spoonful turned out simple, irresistible singles, from the country-based sounds of "Daydream" to the searing rocker "Summer in the City." Featuring a guest turn from South African trumpeter Hugh Masekela, the Byrds took a swipe at the star-making machinery in general (and the Monkees in particular) with 1967's "So You Want to Be a Rock 'n' Roll Star." On the lighter side, '70s tunesmiths Jim Croce ("Time in a Bottle"), John Denver ("Annie's Song") and Bread's David Gates ("If") gave rise to an entire decade's worth of sensitive singer-songwriters.

The smooth sounds of adult-pop radio provided a host of rock veterans with a bona fide shot of success during the 1980s. In late 1981 stadium rockers Foreigner reached the No. 2 spot with their ballad "Waiting for a Girl Like You," then spent the next ten weeks waiting (unsuccessfully) for a girl named Olivia Newton-John ("Physical") to vacate the top spot. Twenty years after penning Spencer Davis Group's Top 10 entry "Gimme Some Lovin'," multi-instrumentalist Steve Winwood hit No. 1 with 1986's "Higher Love," then returned two years later with yet another chart-topper, "Roll with It."

The financial conquests of the Motown, Stax, and Philly International labels during the '60s and '70s irrevocably changed the way the record industry marketed black music to a mass audience—so much so that by the end of the '90s, modern R&B artists came to dominate the pop charts like never before. Balladeers like James Ingram & Patti Austin ("Baby, Come to Me"), Whitney Houston, and Brandy rose to stardom, while the hip-hop movement gave rise to an endless fleet of hitmakers, with notables Lil' Kim and Mya joining new arrivals Christina Aguilera and Pink for a 2001 remake of the LaBelle smash "Lady Marmalade."

As producers became increasingly more involved in the songwriting process, opportunistic songwriters flocked to the country music capital of Nashville, which by the '90s had become one of the last bastions of traditional songwriting in the music industry. Still, hit songwriters like Babyface and Diane Warren continued to prove that opportunities still exist for the "traditional" pop songwriter. Having scored numerous "crossover" country and Latin hits to go with a long list of pop conquests, Warren believes that versatility is the key to success in the new era.

"I really think that a good song with a good lyric and a good story will work for almost anyone," says Warren. "You just have to send it out there—and then sit back and hope for the best."

—David Simons

New England-based author David Simons has been a regular contributor to *Musician*, *Guitar One*, *Acoustic Guitar*, and other publications. His most recent effort, *Roots of Rhythm*, is a multi-part CD series with companion booklet that explores the musical contributions of black Americans from jazz to Motown.

CONTENTS

Africa	Toto	4
Annie's Song	John Denver	10
Baby, Come to Me	Patti Austin with James Ingram	14
Baby, I Love Your Way	Peter Frampton	18
By the Time I Get to Phoenix	Glen Campbell	26
California Girls	The Beach Boys	23
Cathy's Clown	The Everly Brothers	28
Daydream	The Lovin' Spoonful	31
Delta Lady	Joe Cocker	34
(Everything I Do) I Do It for You	Bryan Adams	37
FM	Steely Dan	42
From a Distance	Bette Midler	52
Glory of Love	Peter Cetera	45
Good Lovin'	The Young Rascals	56
Good Vibrations	The Beach Boys	62
Happy Together	The Turtles	68
Hard to Say I'm Sorry	Chicago	72
Higher Love	Steve Winwood	78
Hound Dog	Elvis Presley	65
How Sweet It Is (To Be Loved by You)	James Taylor	86
I Am Woman	Helen Reddy	89
I Got You (I Feel Good)	James Brown	92
I Honestly Love You	Olivia Newton-John	97
I Like It Like That	Chris Kenner	102
I.G.Y. (What a Beautiful World)	Donald Fagen	110
I'll Have to Say I Love You in a Song	Jim Croce	116
I'm Every Woman	Whitney Houston	118
(I've Had) The Time of My Life	Bill Medley & Jennifer Warnes	124
If	Bread	134
If You Leave Me Now	Chicago	105
Imagine	John Lennon	138
In My Life	The Beatles	142
Jack and Diane	John Cougar	145
Joy to the World	Three Dog Night	154
Lady in Red	Chris DeBurgh	164
Lady Marmalade	LaBelle	157
Limbo Rock	Chubby Checker	168
Love Me Tender	Elvis Presley	176
Lowdown	Boz Scaggs	173
Magic Man	Heart	178
Misty Blue	Dorothy Moore	184
Oh, Pretty Woman	Roy Orbison	187
Only the Lonely	The Motels	194
The Rainbow Connection	from The Muppet Movie	197
Rainy Days and Mondays	Carpenters	202
Respect	Aretha Franklin	207
Rock Around the Clock	Bill Haley and His Comets	210
Rocky Mountain High	John Denver	212
Rosanna	Toto	218
Shout	The Isley Brothers	226
(Sittin' On) The Dock of the Bay	Otis Redding	223
So You Want to Be a Rock and Roll Star	The Byrds	240
Summer in the City	The Lovin' Spoonful	246
Superstar	Carpenters	256
Teach Your Children	Crosby, Stills & Nash	249
Tears in Heaven	Eric Clapton	258
Teen Angel	Mark Dinning	268
This Masquerade	George Benson	270
Time in a Bottle	Jim Croce	276
Top of the World	Carpenters	263
Travelin' Man	Ricky Nelson	280
The Twist	Chubby Checker	286
Waiting for a Girl Like You	Foreigner	288
Yesterday	The Beatles	283
You Are So Beautiful	Joe Cocker	294

Africa

Words and Music by
David Paich and Jeff Porcaro

I hear the drums

ech-o-in' to-night.___ She hears on-ly whis-pers of some

qui-et con-ver-sa- - - -tion.

She's com-ing   in,   twelve thir-ty   flight.___
The wild dogs   cry   out   in the   night,___   as

Moon-lit wings___ re-flect the stars___ that guide me toward___ sal-y
they grow rest-less, long-ing for___ some sol-i-tar-___y

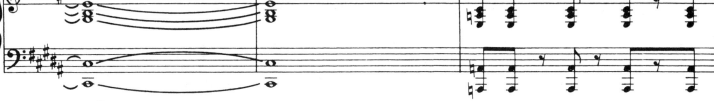

Repeat and fade

Annie's Song

Words and Music by
John Denver

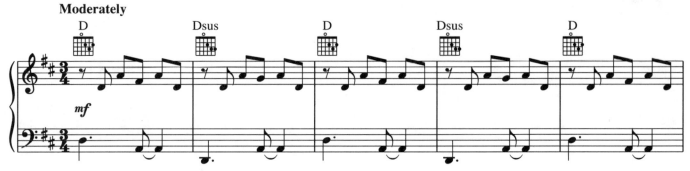

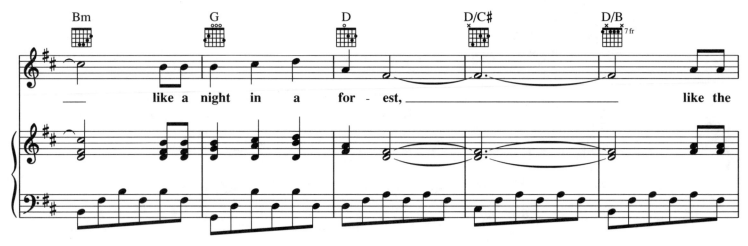

rain, _____ like a storm in the des -

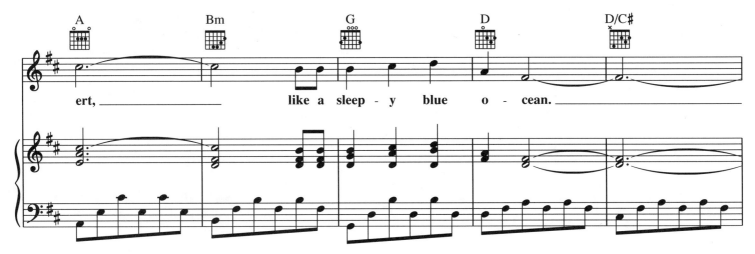

ert, _____ like a sleep - y blue o - cean. _____

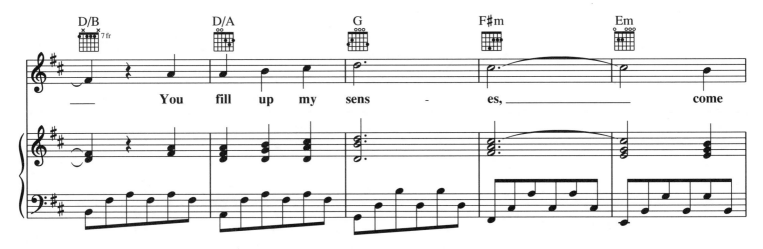

___ You fill up my sens - es, _____ come

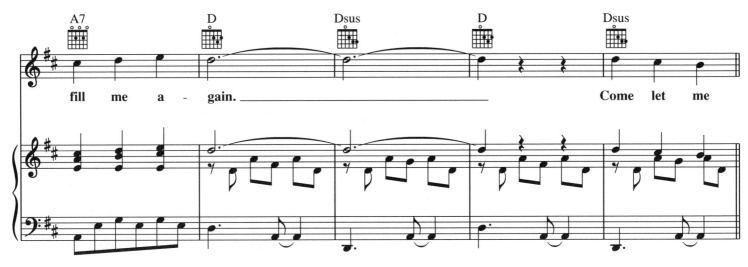

fill me a - gain. _____ Come let me

11

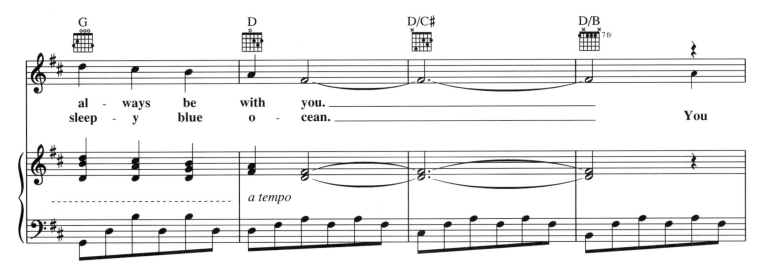

al - ways   be   with   you. _____
sleep - y   blue   o - cean. _____   You

Come   let   me   love   you, _____   come   love   me   a -
fill   up   my   love   sens - es, _____   come   fill   me   a -

gain. _____   You   fill   up   my   gain. _____

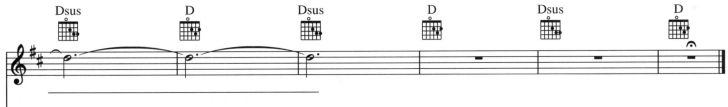

13

Baby, Come to Me

Words and Music by
Rod Temperton

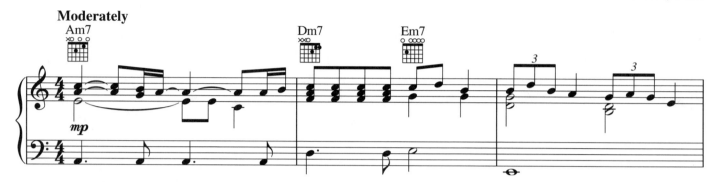

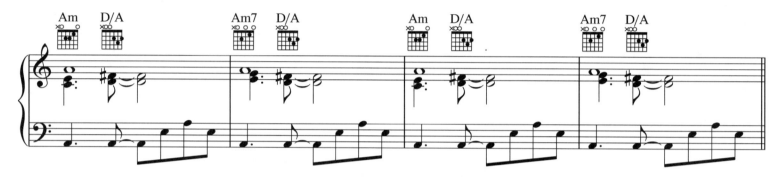

Think-in' back in time,__ when love was on-ly in the mind,__ I re-al-ize
Spend-in' ev-'ry dime__ to keep you talk-in' on the line,__ that's how it was,

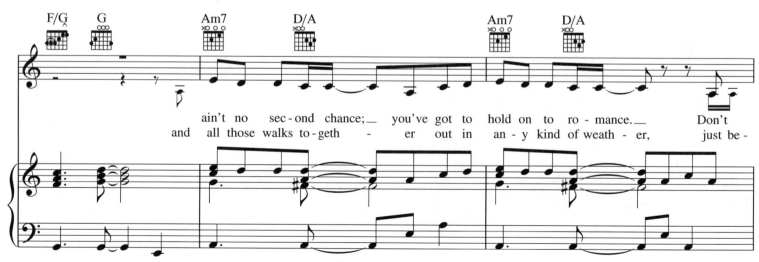

ain't no sec-ond chance;__ you've got to hold on to ro-mance.__ Don't
and all those walks to-geth - er out in an-y kind of weath-er, just be-

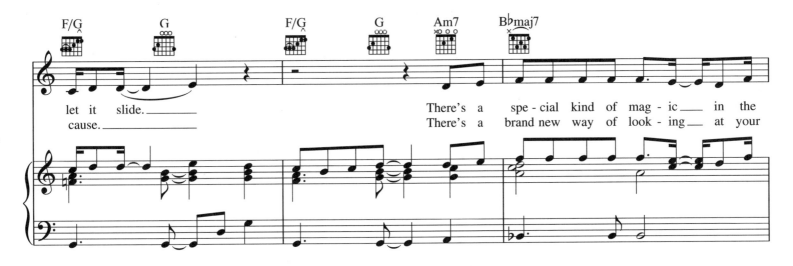

let it slide._____
cause._____

There's a spe-cial kind of mag-ic___ in the
There's a brand new way of look-ing___ at your

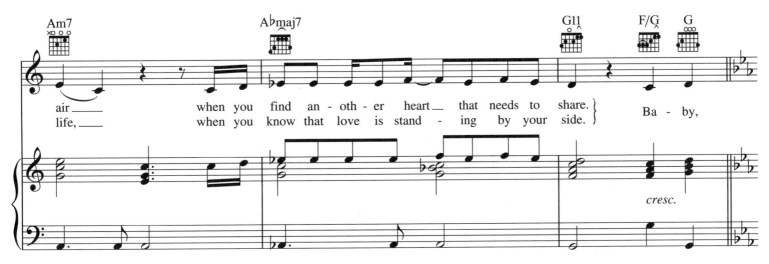

air___
life,___

when you find an-oth-er heart___ that needs to share.
when you know that love is stand - ing by your side.

Ba - by,

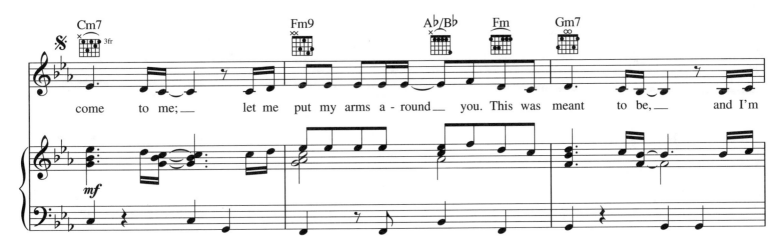

come to me;___ let me put my arms a-round___ you. This was meant to be,___ and I'm

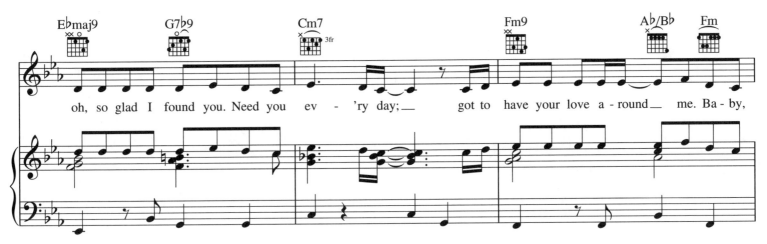

oh, so glad I found you. Need you ev-'ry day;___ got to have your love a-round___ me. Ba - by,

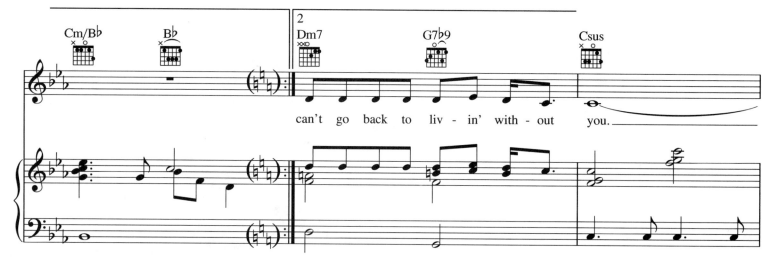

al - ways stay, 'cause I can't go back to liv - in' with - out you.

can't go back to liv - in' with - out you. _____

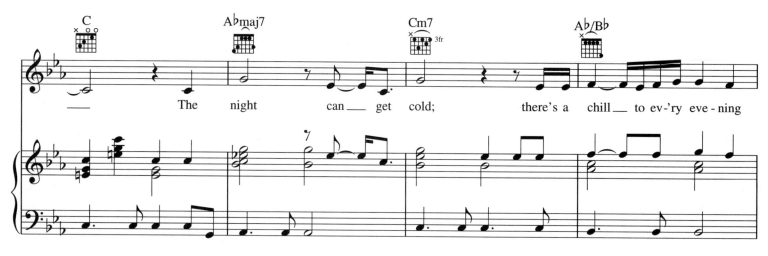

_____ The night can _ get cold; there's a chill _ to ev-'ry eve - ning

when you're all a - lone. _ Don't talk _____ an - y - more, 'cause you

know that I'll__ be here to keep you warm._____ Ba - by,

CODA

can't go back to liv - in' with - out you.
Come to me;__ let me put my arms a - round__ you. This was

meant to be,__ and I'm oh, so glad I found you. Need you ev - 'ry day;__ got to

Repeat and Fade

have your love a - round__ me. Ba - by, al - ways stay, 'cause I can't go back to liv - in' with - out

Baby, I Love Your Way

Words and Music by
Peter Frampton

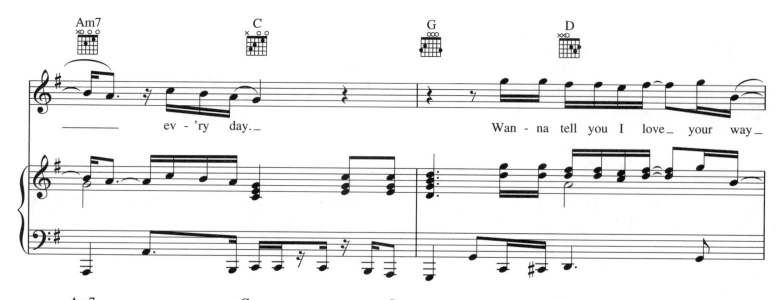

ev - 'ry day.__ Wan - na tell you I love__ your way__

ev - 'ry day.__ Wan - na be with you night__ and day.__

To Coda

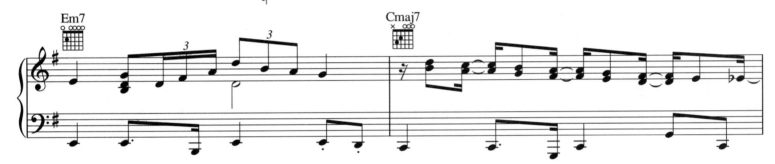

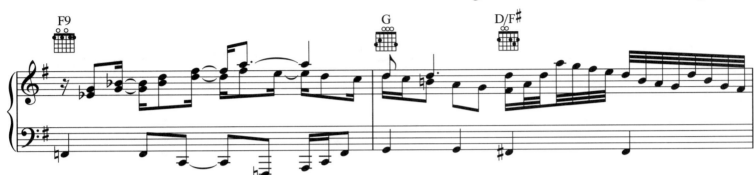

But don't   hes - i - tate, ___   'cause your

love _____

won't ___ wait. _____

D.S. al Coda

Ooh ba-by, I love__ your way__ ev-'ry day.__

Wan-na tell you I love__ your way.____ Ooh._____

Wan-na be with you night__ and day.____

California Girls

Words and Music by
Brian Wilson and Mike Love

Mid - west farm - er's daugh - ters real - ly make you feel al -
been all a - round this great big world, and I've seen all kinds of

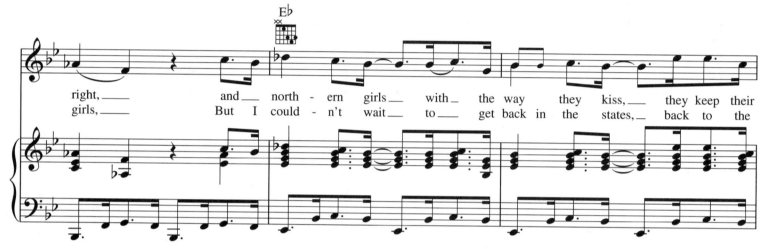

right, ____ and __ north - ern girls __ with __ the way they kiss, __ they keep their
girls, ____ But I could - n't wait __ to __ get back in the states, __ back to the

boy - friends warm at night. ____ }
cut - est girls in the world. ____ }

I wish they all could be __

__ Cal - i - for - nia, I wish they all could be ____ Cal - i - for - nia, I

By the Time I Get to Phoenix

Words and Music by
Jimmy Webb

left that girl _____ so man-y times _____ be-fore.   By the   wall,

that's   all.   By the   time   and time _____

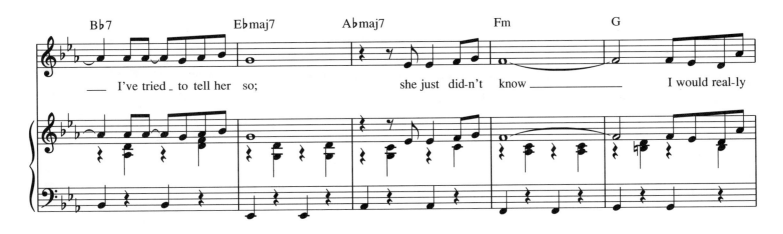

_____ I've tried _ to tell her   so;   she just did-n't   know _____   I would real-ly

go. _____

Cathy's Clown

Words and Music by
Don Everly

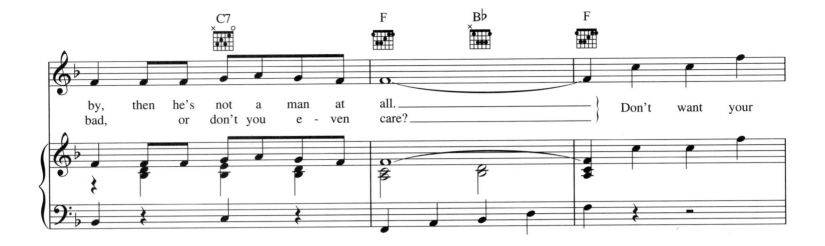

by, then he's not a man at all. _____ } Don't want your
bad, or don't you e - ven care? _____ }

love _____ an - y -

more. Don't want your kiss -

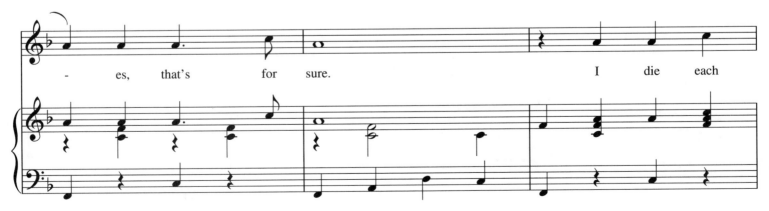

- es, that's for sure. I die each

Dm   Bb

time _____ I hear this sound.

C7   F

Here he comes. _____ That's Cath - y's

1.

clown. _____ When you see me shed a

2.

clown. _____

Daydream

Words and Music by
John Sebastian

Moderately

C
What a day for a day - dream, _____
I've been hav - ing a sweet _____ dream, _____

A7

Dm7
What a day for a
I've been dream - in' since I

G7
day - dream - in' boy. _____
woke up to - day. _____

C
And I'm lost in a day - dream, _____
It's star - ring me and my sweet _____ dream, _____

A7

Dm7
dream - in' 'bout my
'cause she's the one makes me

G11 **G7**
bun - dle of joy. _____
feel _____ this way. _____

F **D7/F♯**
And ev - en if time ain't real - ly
And ev - en if time _____ is pass - ing

3. *Whistle*
   Whistle
   Whistle
   Whistle
   And you can be sure that if you're feelin' right,
   A daydream will last till long into the night.
   Tomorrow at breakfast you may pick up your ears,
   Or you may be daydreamin' for a thousand years.

Delta Lady

Words and Music by
Leon Russell

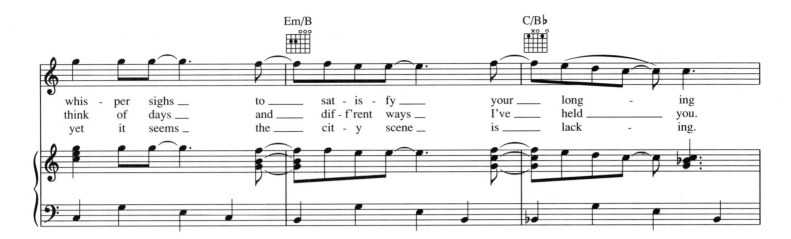

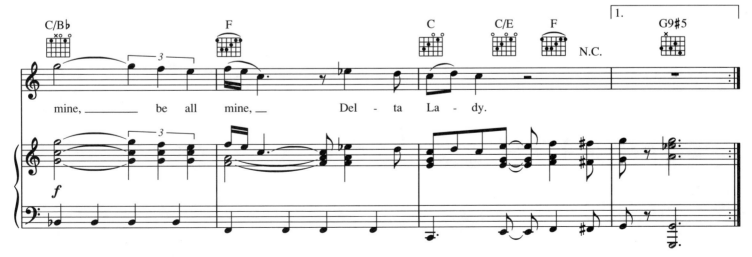

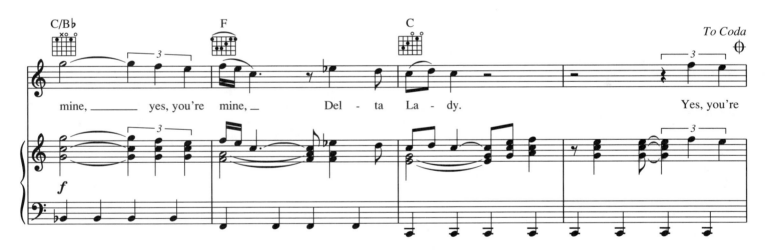

Oh, _____ when I'm home __ a - gain __ in Eng - land,

I'll ___ think of you, ___ love. ___   Be - cause I

D.S. al Coda

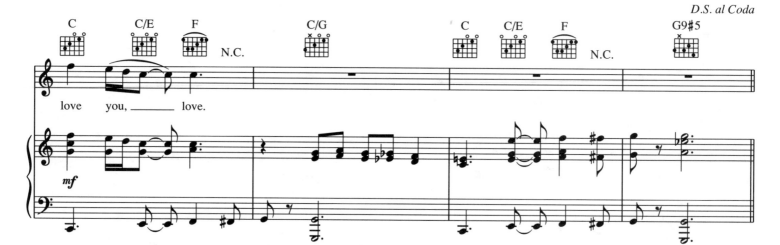

love you, _____ love.

Coda

Repeat and fade

mine, _____ be all mine, _ Del - ta La - dy.   Yes, you're
mine, _____ yes, you're mine, _ Del - ta La - dy.   Yes, you're

(Everything I Do)
I Do It for You

from the Motion Picture ROBIN HOOD: PRINCE OF THIEVES

Words and Music by Bryan Adams,
Robert John Lange and Michael Kamen

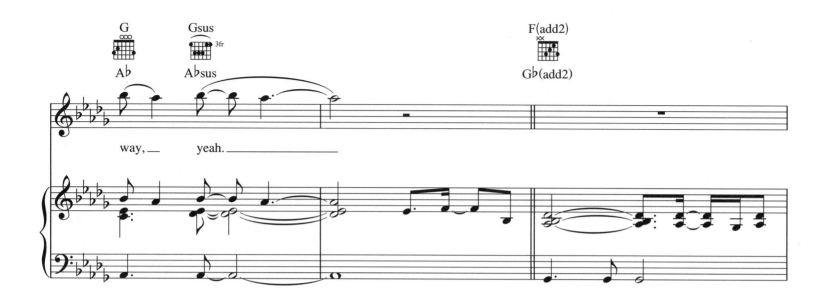

way,___ yeah._____

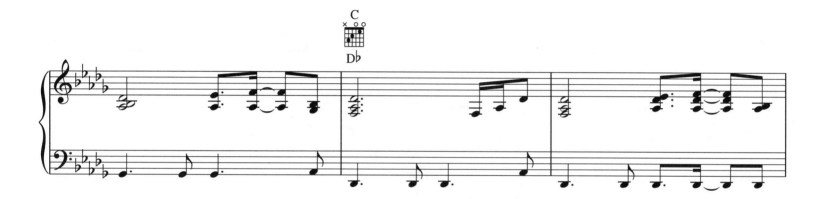

Oh, you can't tell me it's not worth try - ing for. I can't

help it, there's noth-ing I want more. Yeah,__ I would fight__ for you,__ I'd

lie__ for you,__ walk the mile for you,__ yeah,__ I'd

die for__ you.__ You know it's true, ev-'ry-thing I

do, oh,___ oh, I do it for__ you.

FM

from the film FM

Words and Music by
Walter Becker and Donald Fagen

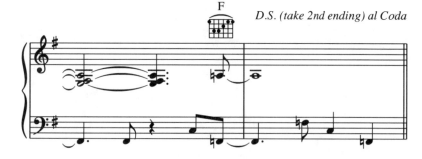

Glory of Love
Theme from KARATE KID PART II

Words and Music by
David Foster, Peter Cetera
and Diane Nini

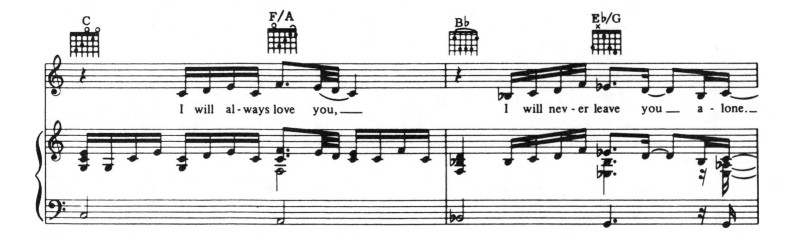

I will al-ways love you, ___ I will nev-er leave you ___ a-lone. ___

Some-times I just for-get, say things I might re-gret, ___
You keep me stand-ing tall, you help me through it all, ___

it breaks my heart ___ to see ___ you cry ___ ing.
I'm al-ways strong ___ when you're ___ be-side me.

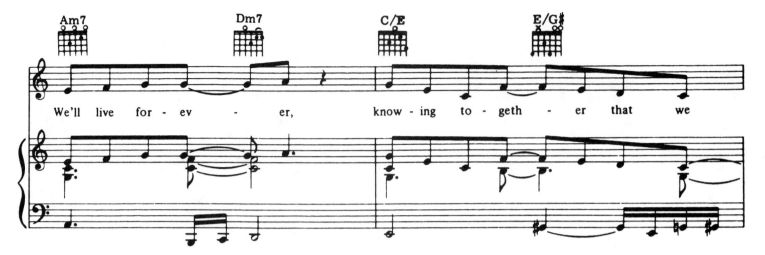

We'll live for - ev - er, know - ing to - geth - er that we

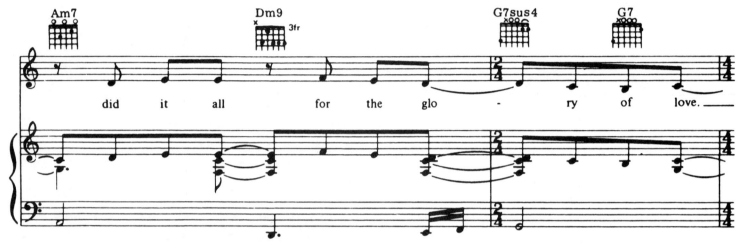

did it all for the glo - ry of love. ____

1.

2.

Just like a knight in shin - ing ar - mor, from a long time a - go,

just in time I will save the day, — take you to my cas - tle far a - way. _____

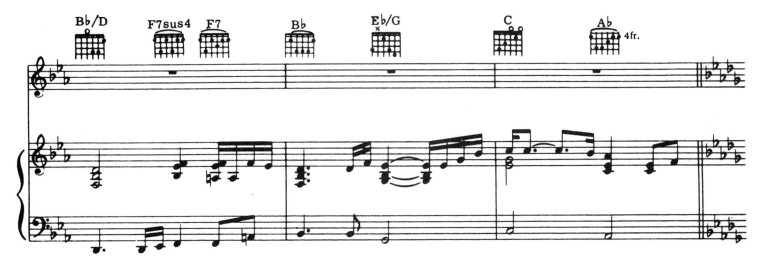

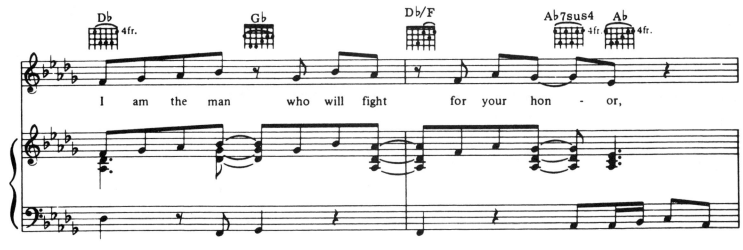

I am the man who will fight for your hon - or,

I'll be the he - ro that you're _____ dream - ing of. _____ We're

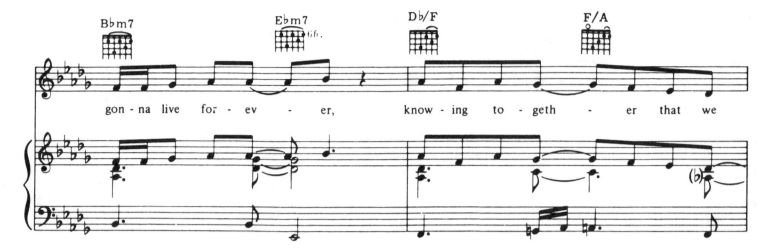

gon -na live for - ev - er, knowing to - geth - er that we

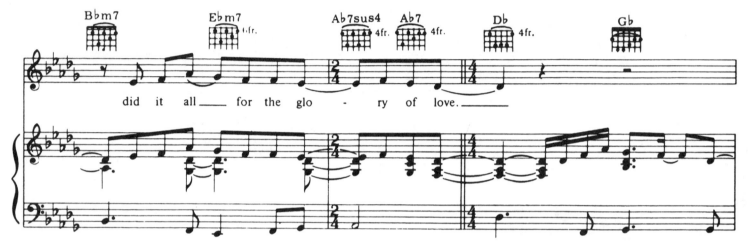

did it all___ for the glo - ry of love.___

We'll live for - ev - er, know - ing to - geth - er that we

did it all _____ for the glo - ry of love. _____

We did _____ it all _____ for love. _____

Repeat and fade

We did _____ it all _____ for love. _____

We did _____ it all _____ for love. _____

From a Distance

Words and Music by
Julie Gold

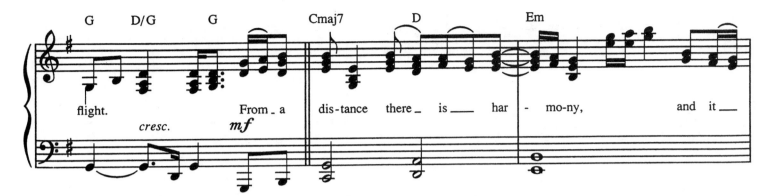

flight. *cresc.* *mf* From a dis-tance there is har-mo-ny, and it

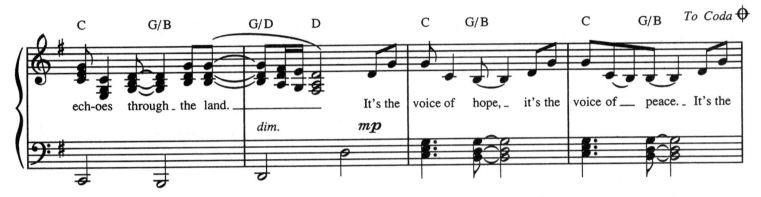

To Coda ⊕

ech-oes through the land. *dim.* *mp* It's the voice of hope, it's the voice of peace. It's the

1.

voice of ev - ery man.

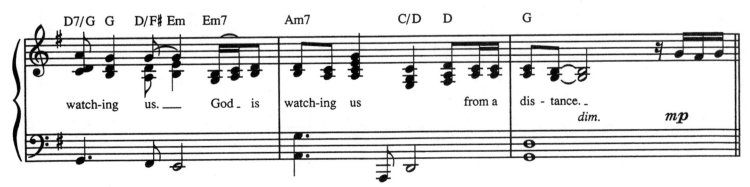

D.S. 𝄋 2. *Bridge:*

2. From a man. *cresc.* *mf* God is watch-ing us. God is

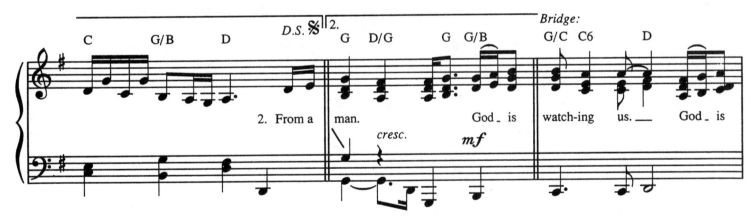

watch-ing us. God is watch-ing us from a dis - tance. *dim.* *mp*

53

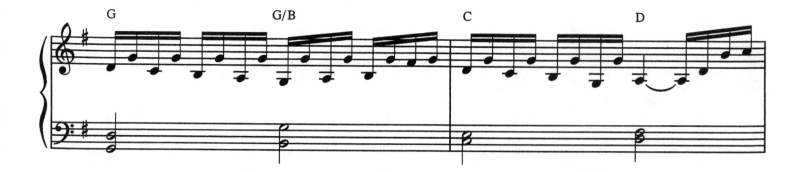

D.S. 𝄋 al Coda

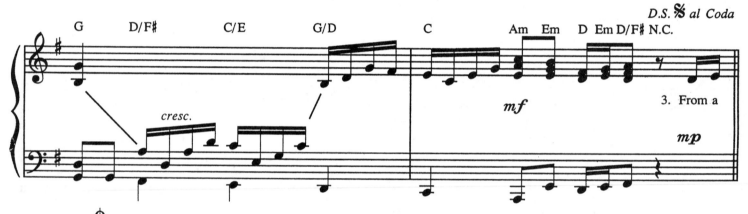

3. From a

heart _____ of ev - ery __ man. _____ It's the

hope of __ hopes, __ it's the love of __ loves. __ This is the song __ of __ ev - ery

man. _____ And God _ is | watch-ing us. _ God _ is | watch-ing us _ God _ is

watch-ing us | from a _ dis - tance. _____ | Oh, God is _ watch-ing us _____ from a

dis - tance.

Verse 2:
From a distance, we all have enough,
And no one is in need.
There are no guns, no bombs, no diseases,
No hungry mouths to feed.
From a distance, we are instruments
Marching in a common band;
Playing songs of hope, playing songs of peace,
They're the songs of every man.
(To Bridge:)

Verse 3:
From a distance, you look like my friend
Even though we are at war.
From a distance I just cannot comprehend
What all this fighting is for.
From a distance there is harmony
And it echos through the land.
It's the hope of hopes, it's the love of loves.
It's the heart of every man.

Good Lovin'

Words and Music by
Rudy Clark and Arthur Resnick

Well, I was feel - ing
So come on ba - by,

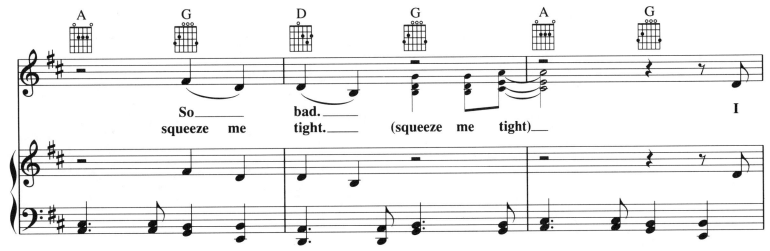

So_____ bad._____ I
squeeze me tight.____ (squeeze me tight)____

asked my fam - 'ly doc - tor just what I had.
Don't you want your Bob - by to be all right? (be all right)_

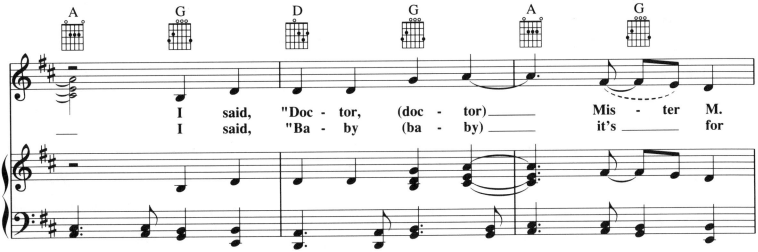

_____ I said, "Doc - tor, (doc - tor)_____ Mis - ter M.
I said, "Ba - by (ba - by)_____ it's _____ for

(scat on "doo's")

60

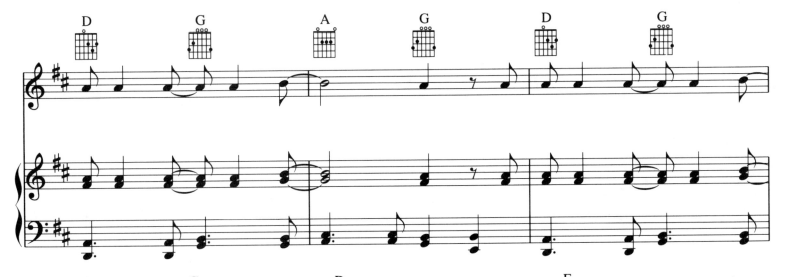

D.S. al Coda

Good

CODA

Repeat ad lib.
and Fade

love.   Good   good lov - in', ba - by, Good

Good Vibrations

Words and Music by
Brian Wilson and Mike Love

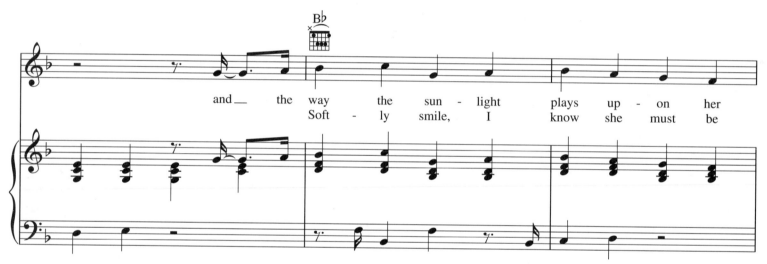

gen - tle word _____ on ___ the wind that lifts her
in her eyes, _____ she ___ goes with me lifts to a

per - fume through the air. _____
blos - som world. _____

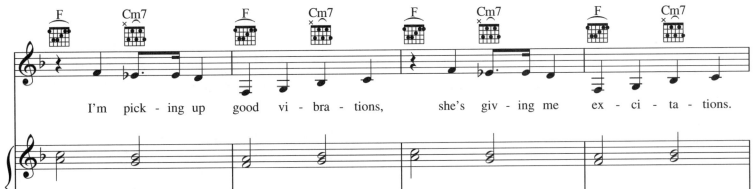

I'm pick - ing up good vi - bra - tions, she's giv - ing me ex - ci - ta - tions.

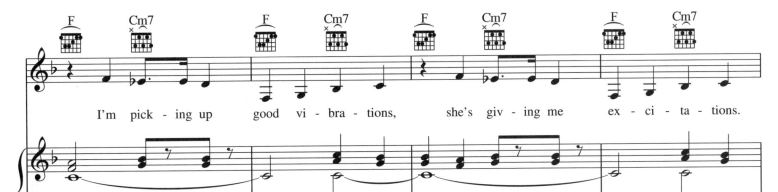

I'm pick - ing up good vi - bra - tions, she's giv - ing me ex - ci - ta - tions.

I'm pick - ing up good vi - bra - tions, she's giv - ing me

ex - ci - ta - tions. I'm pick - ing up good vi - bra - tions,

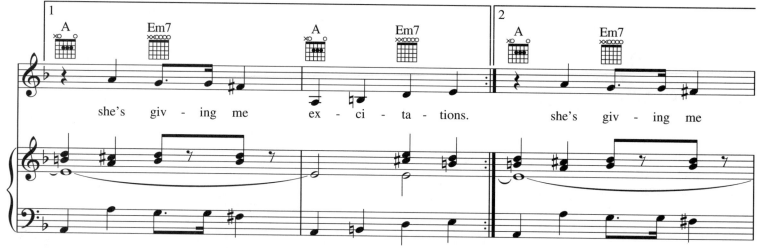

she's giv - ing me ex - ci - ta - tions. she's giv - ing me

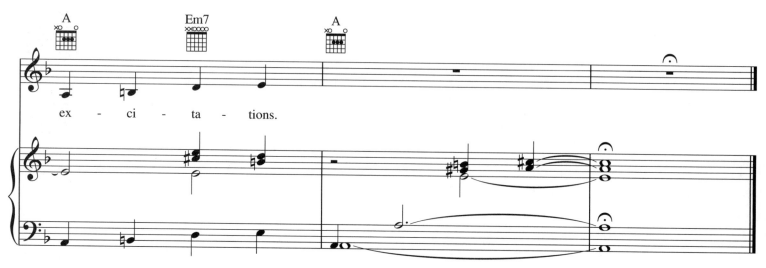

ex - ci - ta - tions.

Hound Dog

Words and Music by
Jerry Leiber and Mike Stoller

Happy Together

Words and Music by
Garry Bonner and Alan Gordon

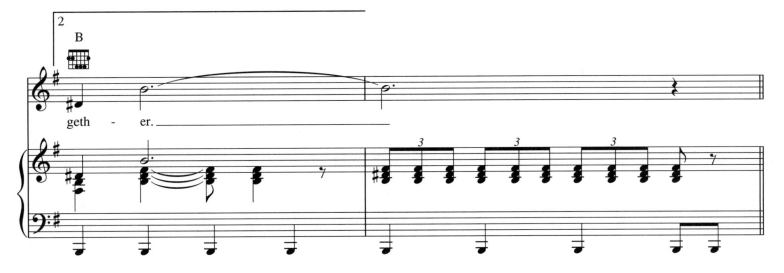

geth - er. _____

I can see me lov - in' no - bod - y but you for all my life.__

When you're with me, ba - by, the skies__ 'll be

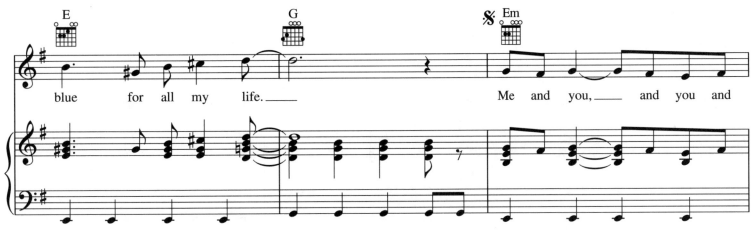

blue for all my life.____ Me and you,____ and you and

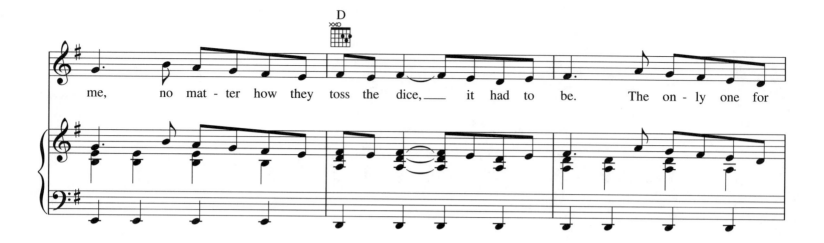

me, no mat - ter how they toss the dice,____ it had to be. The on - ly one for

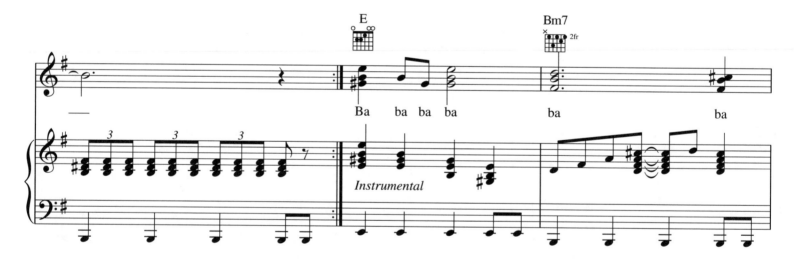

me is you,____ and you for me, so hap - py to - geth - er.____

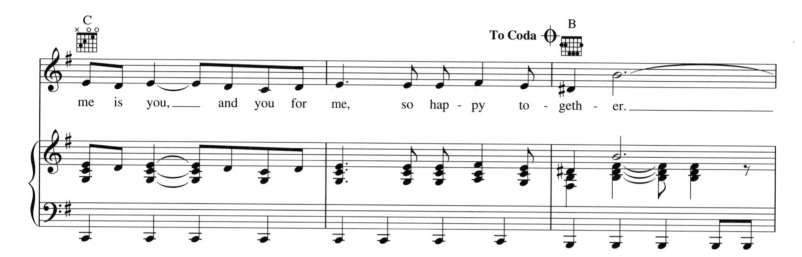

Ba ba ba ba   ba   ba

Instrumental

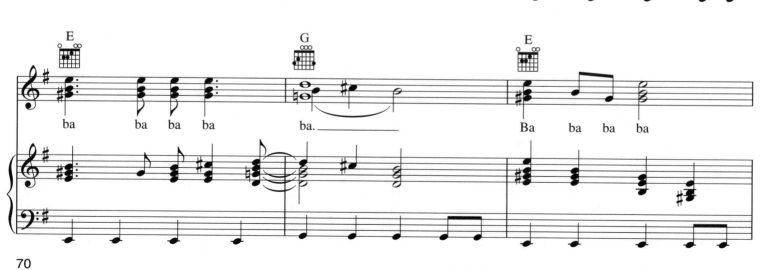

ba   ba ba ba   ba.____   Ba   ba ba ba

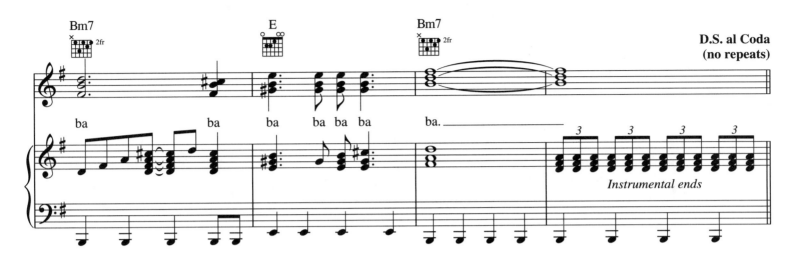

D.S. al Coda (no repeats)

Instrumental ends

ba ba ba ba ba ba ba.

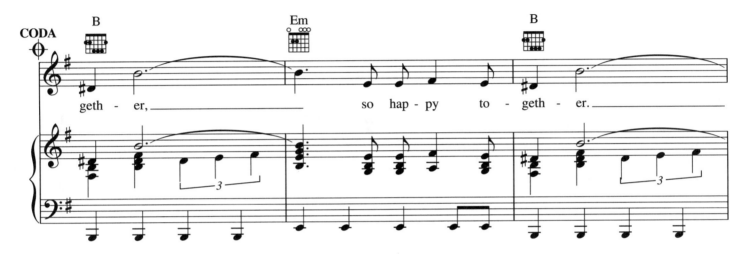

CODA

geth - er, _____ so hap - py to - geth - er. _____

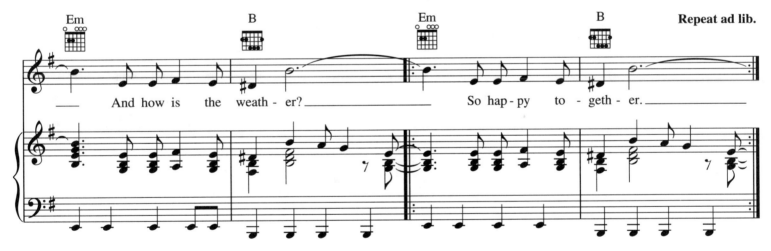

Repeat ad lib.

And how is the weath - er? _____ So hap - py to - geth - er. _____

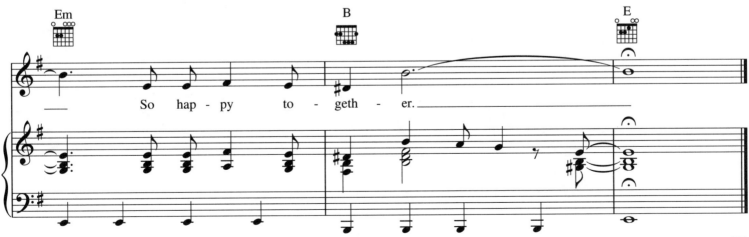

So hap - py to - geth - er. _____

Hard to Say I'm Sorry

Words and Music by
Peter Cetera and David Foster

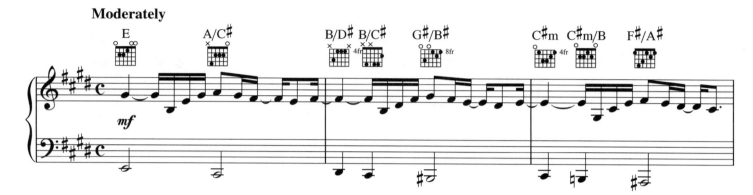

Ev - 'ry - bod - y needs a lit - tle time a - way,___ I heard her say,___

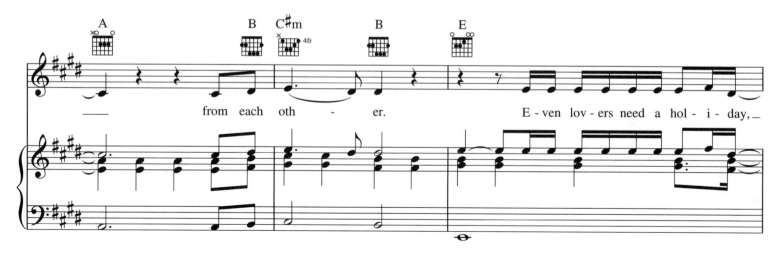

___ from each oth - er. E - ven lov - ers need a hol - i - day,___

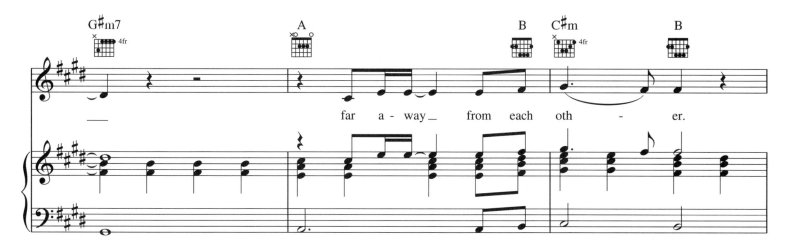

far a - way___ from each oth - - er.

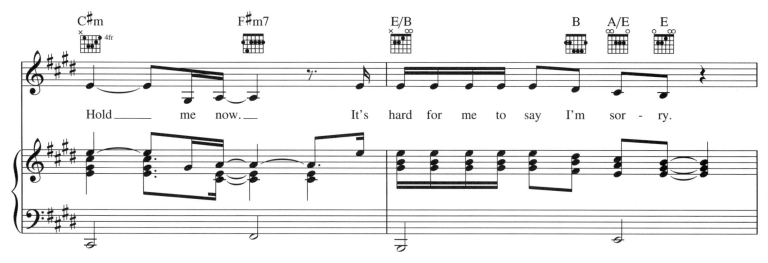

Hold___ me now.___ It's hard for me to say I'm sor - ry.

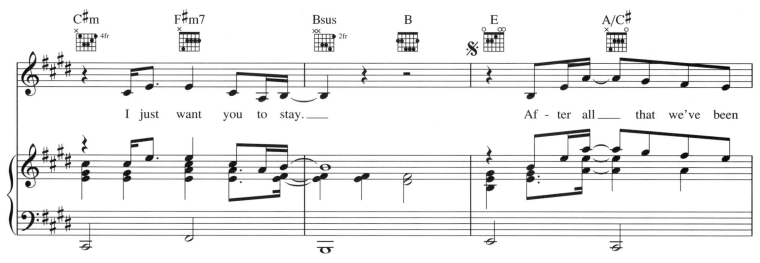

I just want you to stay.___ Af - ter all___ that we've been

through, I will make it up___ to you.___ I'll prom - ise to.

And af - ter all that's been said_____ and done, you're just___

_____ the part_____ of me___ I can't_____ let go.

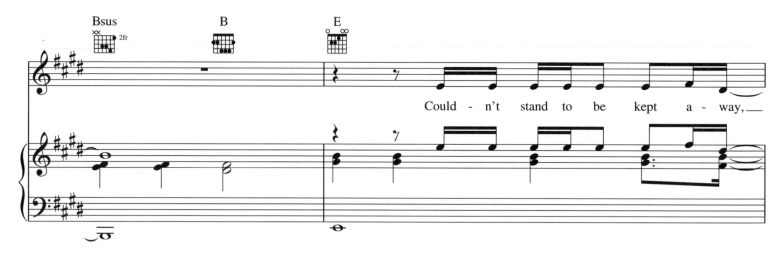

Could - n't stand to be kept a - way,___

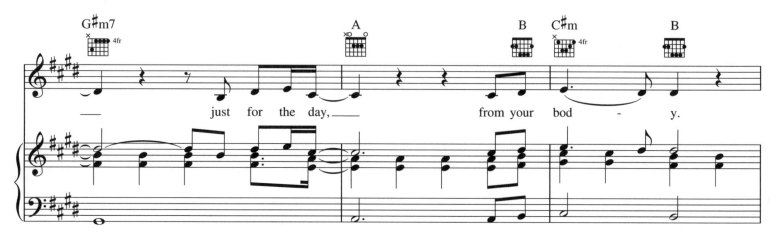

just for the day,_____ from your bod___ - y.

74

Would -n't wan-na be swept a - way,_____

far a - way, from the one that I love.

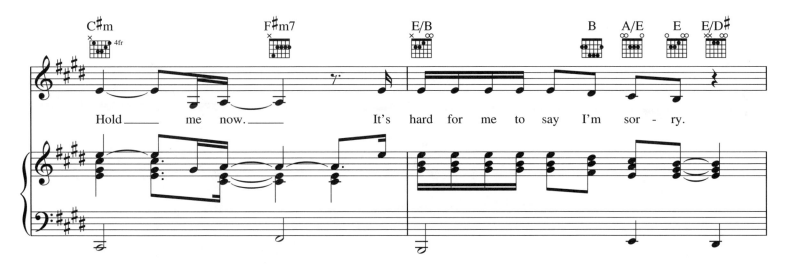

Hold_____ me now._____ It's hard for me to say I'm sor - ry.

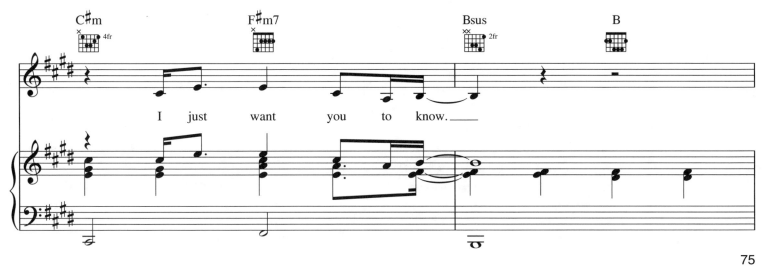

I just want you to know._____

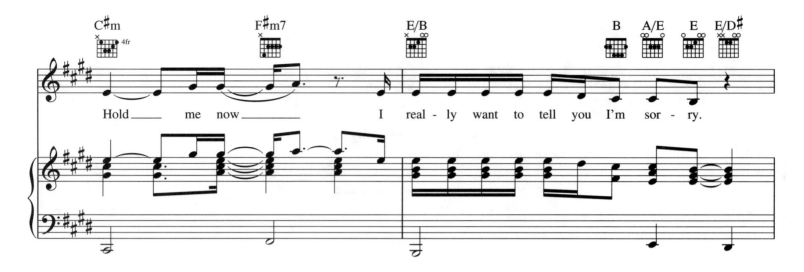

Hold___ me now___ I real - ly want to tell you I'm sor - ry.

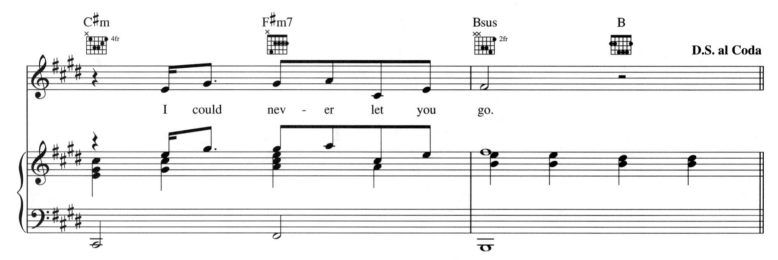

I could nev - er let you go.

D.S. al Coda

CODA

___ the part___ of me___ I can't___ let go.

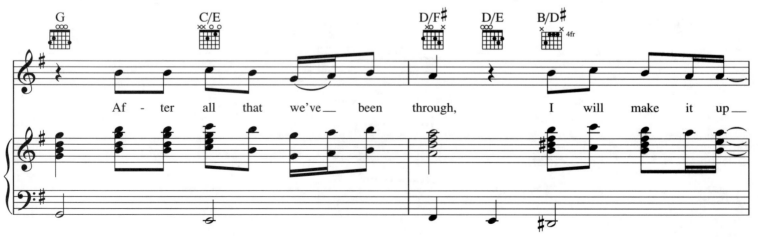

Af - ter all that we've___ been through, I will make it up___

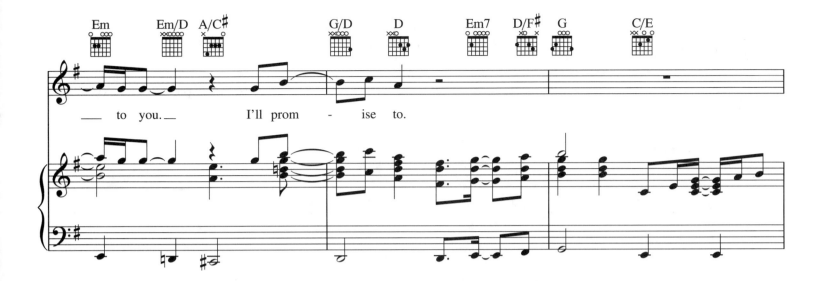

to you. I'll prom - ise to.

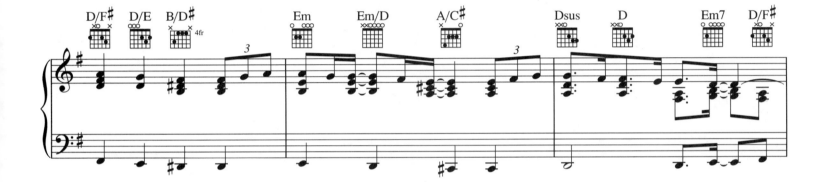

You're gon-na be the luck - y one.

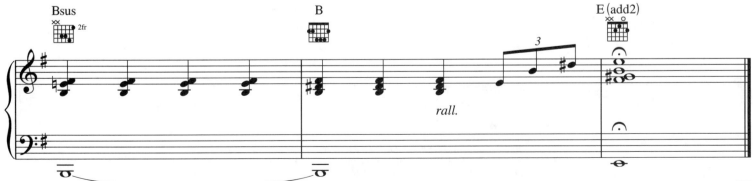

rall.

Higher Love

Words and Music by
Will Jennings and Steve Winwood

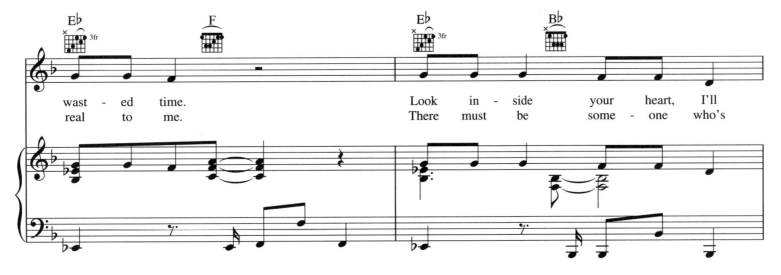

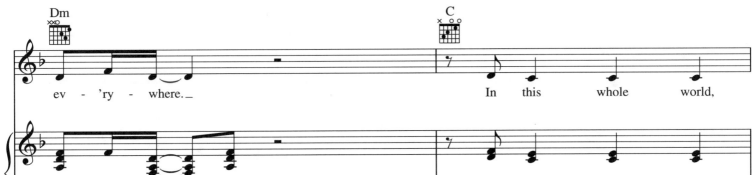

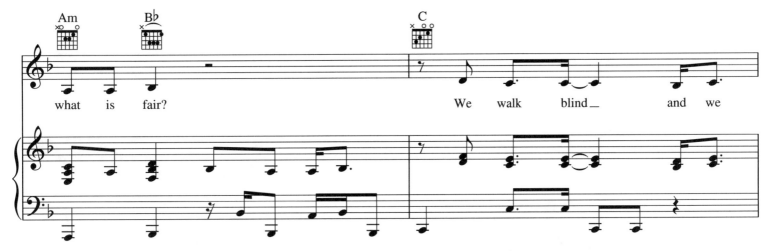

try to see, _____ falling be - hind in what

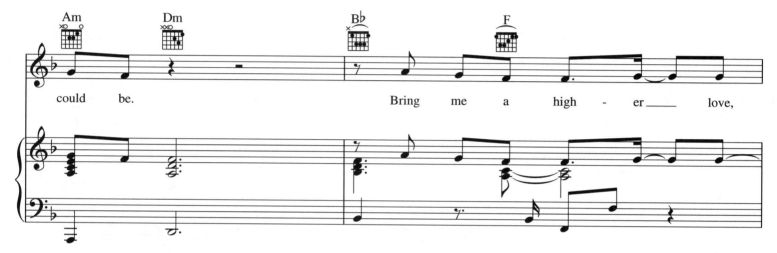

could be. Bring me a high - er _____ love,

bring me a high - er _____ love,

woah. _____ Bring me a high - er _____ love.

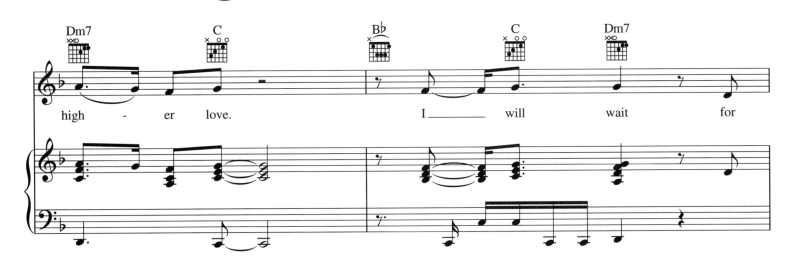

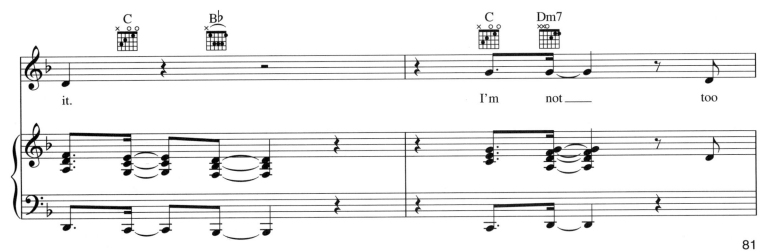

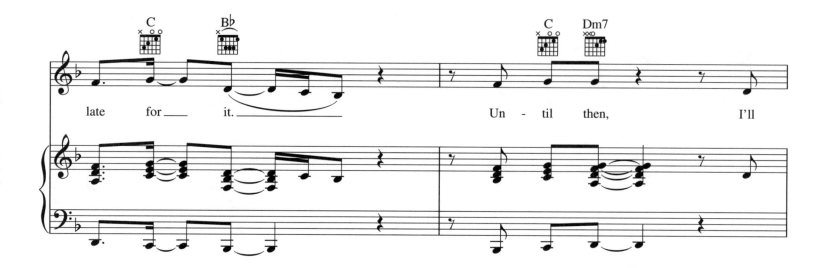

late for ___ it. ___ Un - til then, I'll

sing my song to cheer ___ the

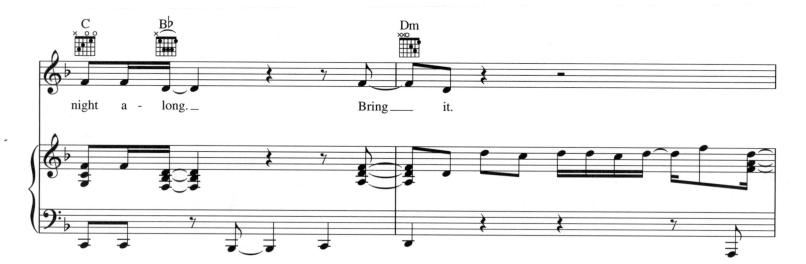

night a - long. ___ Bring ___ it.

strong it could be. _____

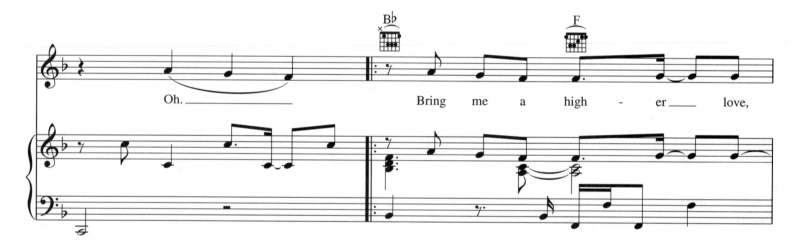

Oh. _____

Bring me a high - er ____ love,

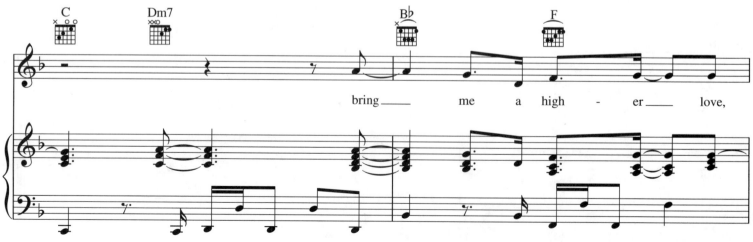

bring ____ me a high - er ____ love,

woah. ___

Bring me a high-er ___ love,

bring me a high-er ___ love. ___

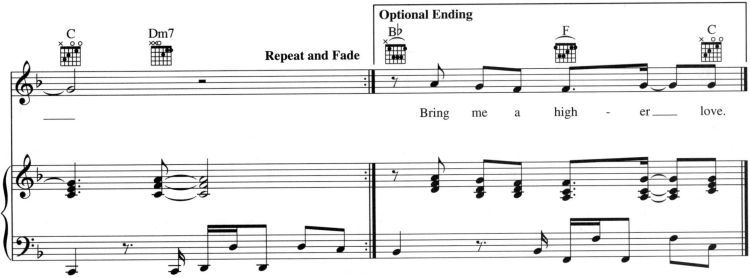

Repeat and Fade

Optional Ending

___

Bring me a high-er ___ love.

How Sweet It Is
(To Be Loved by You)

Words and Music by
Edward Holland, Lamont Dozier
and Brian Holland

You were bet-ter to me than I was to my-self, ___ for me there's_you and there ain't no-bo-dy else.__I want to stop and thank you ba-by; ___ I want to stop and thank you ba-by, yes I do, How sweet it is ___ to be loved by you.

Coda

repeat and fade

I Am Woman

Words by Helen Reddy

Music by Ray Burton

ev - er gon - na keep___ me down a - gain. Oh,___ yes, I am wise___ but it's wis -

- dom born of pain._____ Yes, I paid the price,___ but look how much___ I gained.___ If I

have to___ I can___ do an - y - thing.___ I am strong, I am in -

To Coda ⊕

vin - ci - ble,___ I am wom - an. ___

I Got You

(I Feel Good)

Words and Music by
James Brown

Woh!   I feel   good. _____

I knew that I would _____ now.
Ah, sug - ar and spice. _____

I feel _____ good.
I feel _____ nice.

I knew that I would___ now. So good,
Ah, sug - ar and spice.___ So nice,

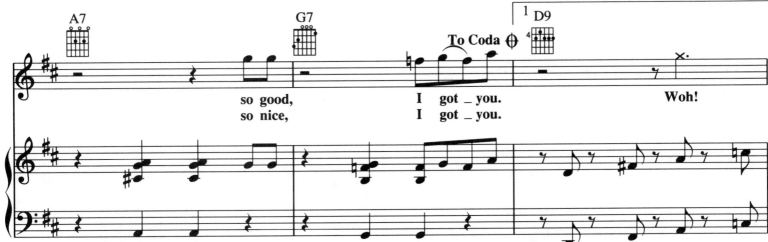

so good, I got _ you. Woh!
so nice, I got _ you.

I feel nice._

no chord

When I hold you ___ in my arms I
know that I can do no wrong. _____ and
when I hold ___ you in ___ my arms my { love won't do you no harm.
                                          love can't do me no harm. ___
___ } And I feel _____ nice. _____ Ah, sug - ar and spice.

94

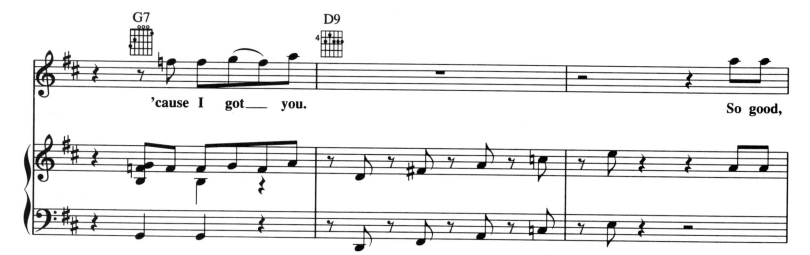

I Honestly Love You

Words and Music by
Peter Allen and Jeff Barry

Moderately slow

May - be I hang a - round_ here a lit - tle more than I should; we
You don't_ have to an - swer; I see it in your eyes.

both know I got some - where else_ to go. But
May - be it was bet - ter left_ un - said. But

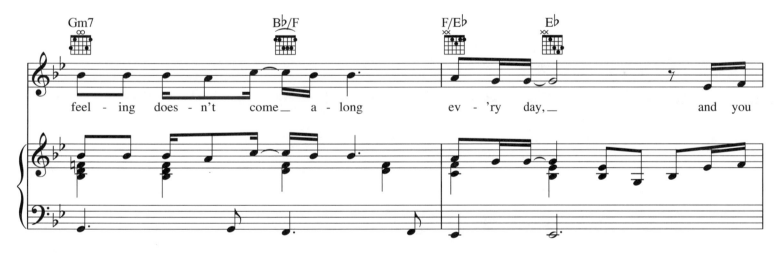

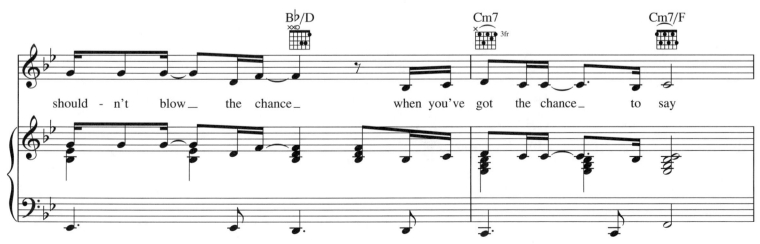

I love you.   *(Spoken:) I love you.*

I hon - est - ly love __ you.

If we both __ were born _____ in an - oth - er place and time, this

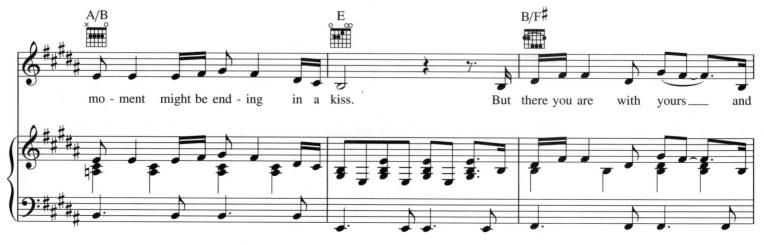

mo - ment might be end - ing in a kiss.   But there you are with yours __ and

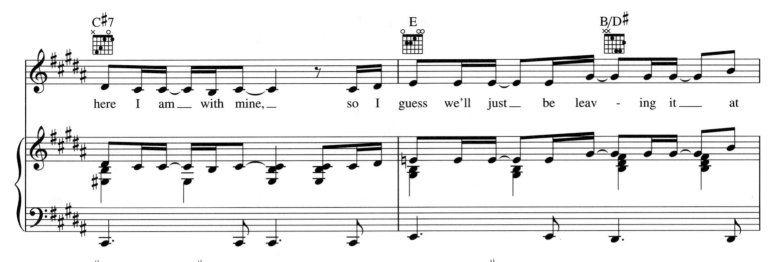

here I am __ with mine, __ so I guess we'll just __ be leav - ing it __ at

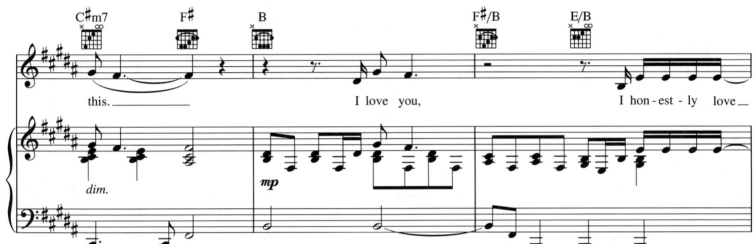

this. __ I love you, I hon - est - ly love __

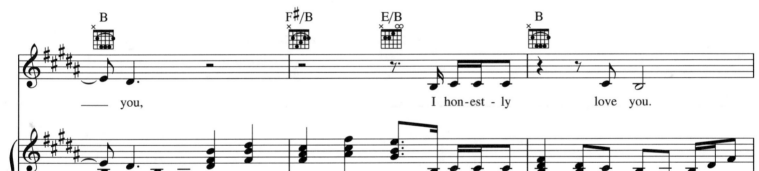

__ you, I hon - est - ly love you.

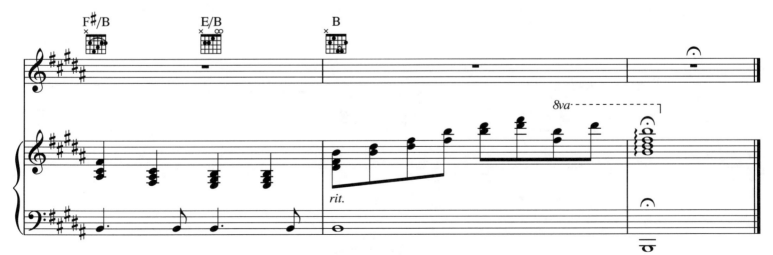

I Like It Like That

Words and Music by
Chris Kenner

If You Leave Me Now

Words and Music by
Peter Cetera

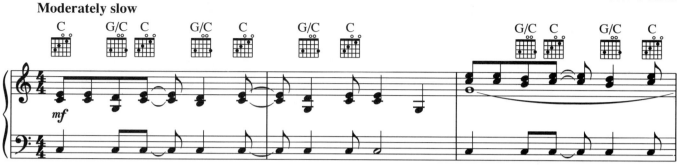

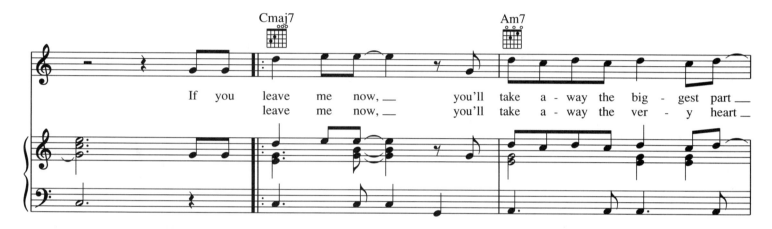

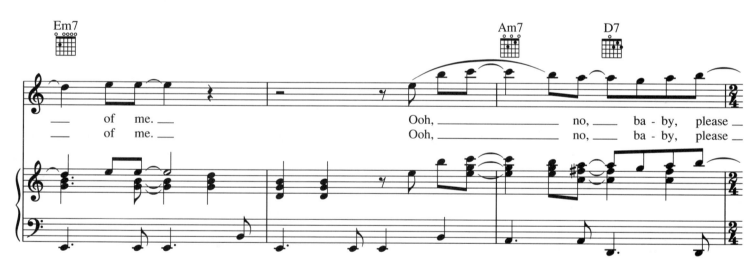

Lyrics:

If you leave me now, ___ you'll take a way the big - gest part ___
leave me now, ___ you'll take a way the ver - y heart ___

___ of me. ___ Ooh, ___ no, ___ ba - by, please ___
___ of me. ___ Ooh, ___ no, ___ ba - by, please ___

___ don't go. ___ And if you
___ don't go. ___ Ooh, ___

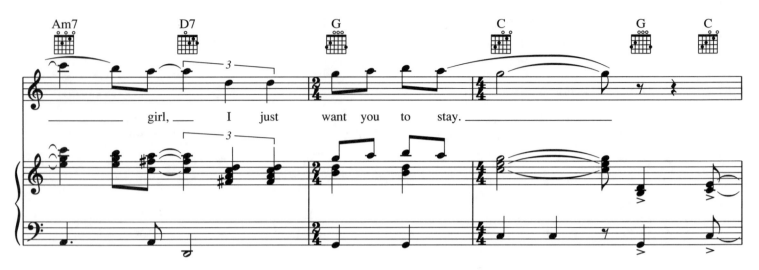

girl, ___ I just want you to stay. _____

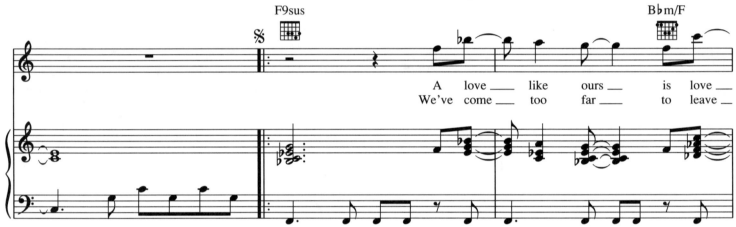

A love ___ like ours ___ is love ___
We've come ___ too far ___ to leave ___

___ that's hard ___ to find. _____
___ it all ___ be - hind. _____

How could we let ___
How could we end ___

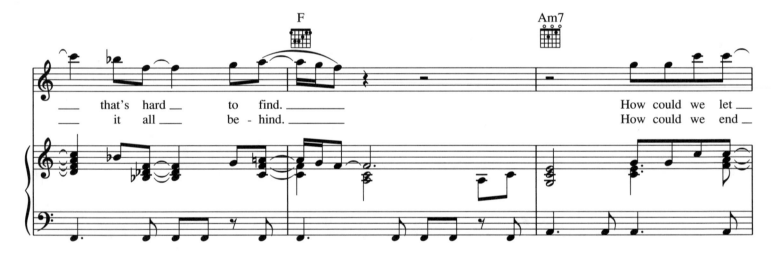

___ it ___ slip ___ a - way? _____
___ it all ___ this way? _

When to - mor -

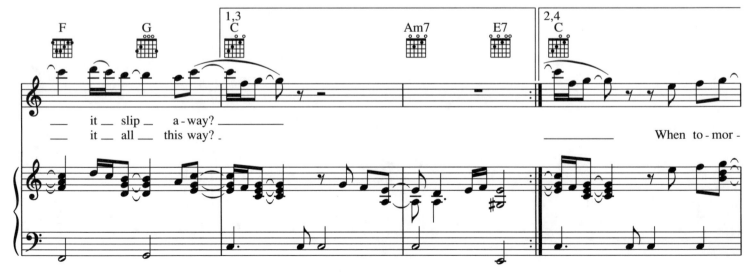

-row comes, ___ then we'll both ___ re - gret ___ the things we said ___ to - day. __

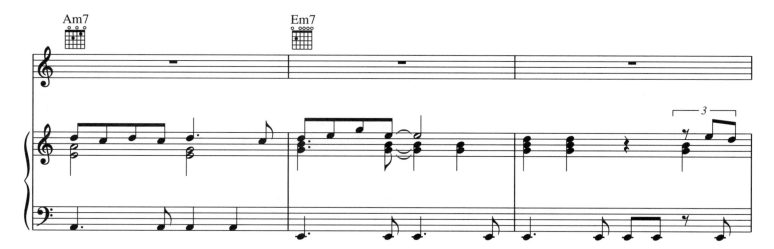

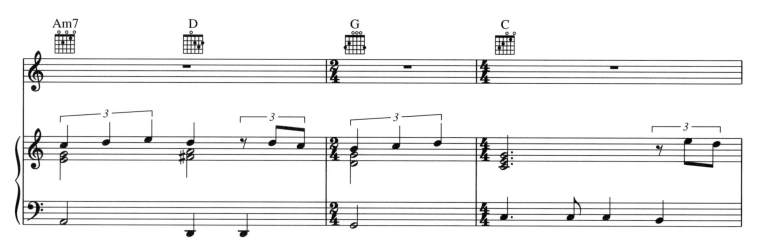

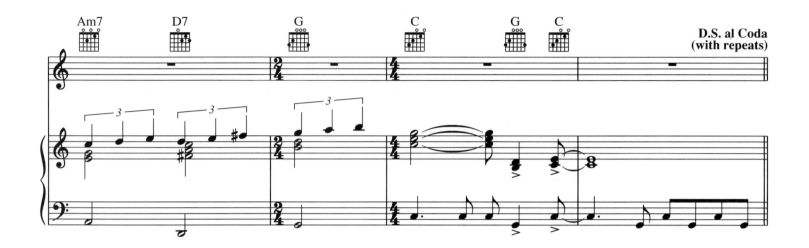

D.S. al Coda
(with repeats)

CODA

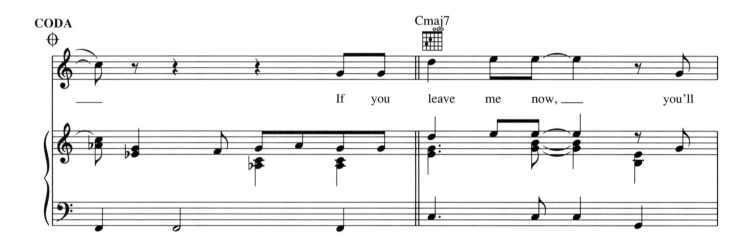

If you leave me now, ___ you'll

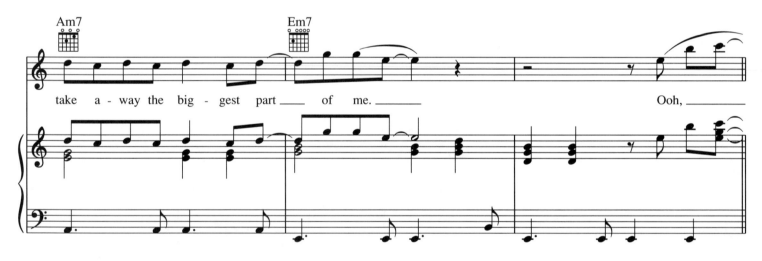

take a - way the big - gest part ___ of me. ___ Ooh, ___

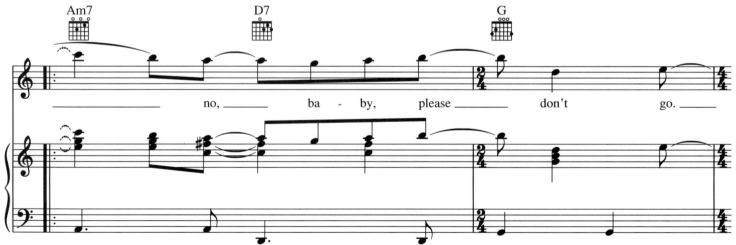

___ no, ___ ba - by, please ___ don't go. ___

Ooh, _____ girl, _____ just
Ooh, ma - ma, _____ I just

got to have _ you by my side. _____
got to have _ your lov - in'. _____

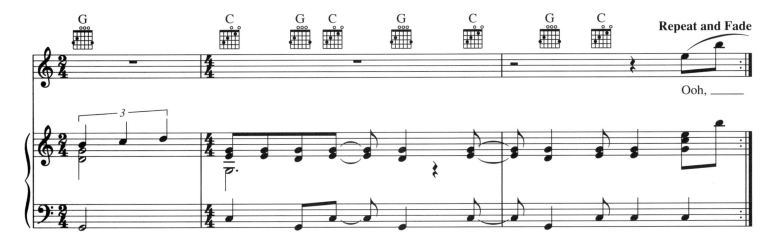

Repeat and Fade

Ooh, _____

I.G.Y.
(What a Beautiful World)

Words and Music by
Donald Fagen

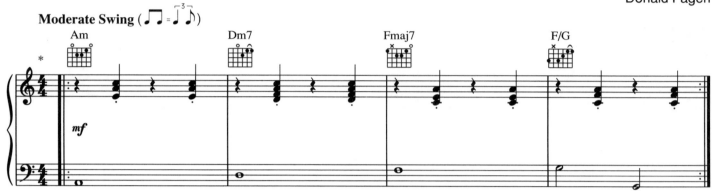

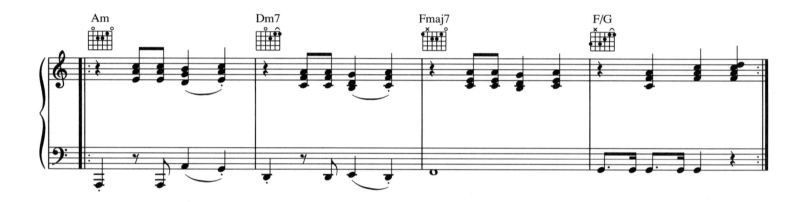

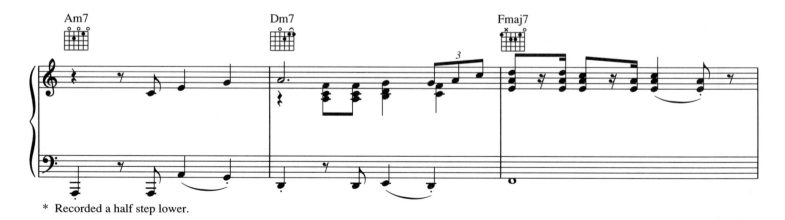

* Recorded a half step lower.

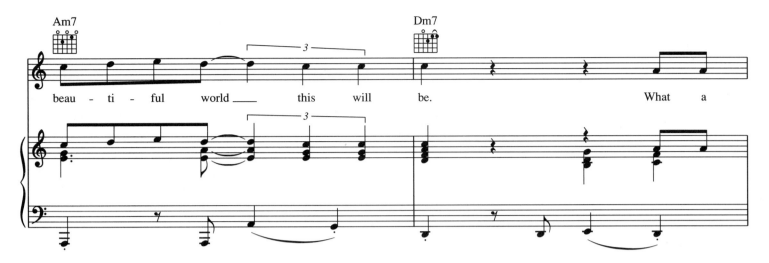

beau - ti - ful world ___ this will be. What a

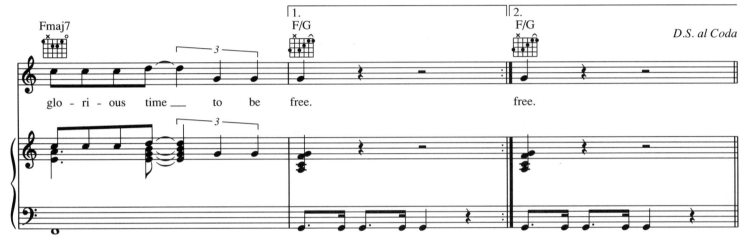

glo - ri - ous time ___ to be free. free.

D.S. al Coda

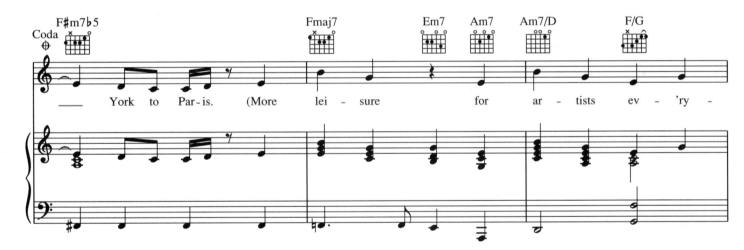

___ York to Par - is. (More lei - sure for ar - tists ev - 'ry -

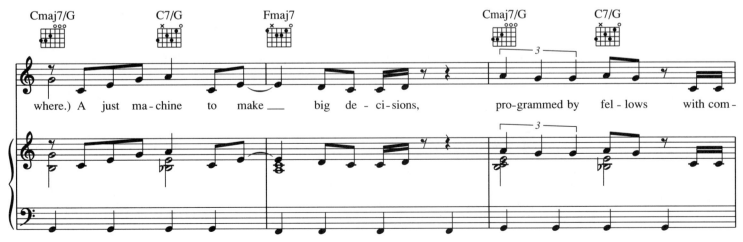

where.) A just ma - chine to make ___ big de - ci - sions, pro - grammed by fel - lows with com -

113

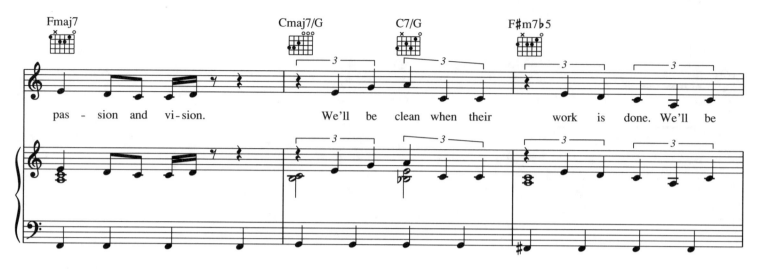

pas - sion and vi - sion. We'll be clean when their work is done. We'll be

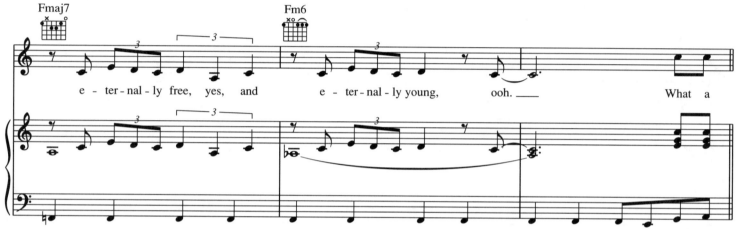

e - ter - nal - ly free, yes, and e - ter - nal - ly young, ooh. ___ What a

beau - ti - ful world __ this will be. What a glo - ri - ous time __ to be

free. What a beau - ti - ful world __ this will be. What a

glo - ri - ous time ___ to be free. What a free.

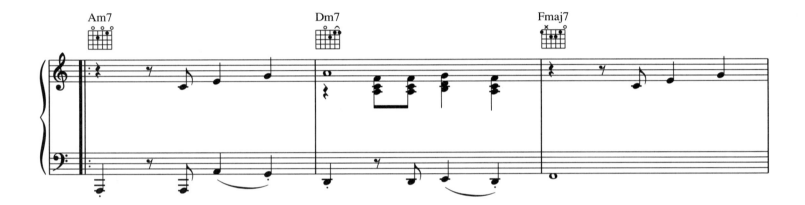

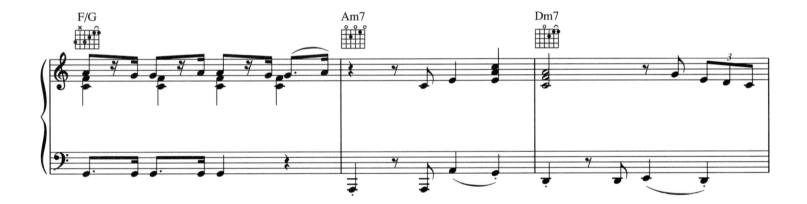

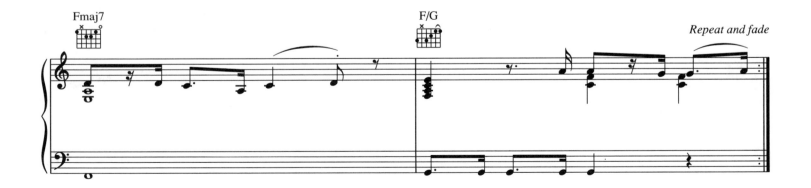

Repeat and fade

I'll Have to Say I Love You in a Song

Words and Music by
Jim Croce

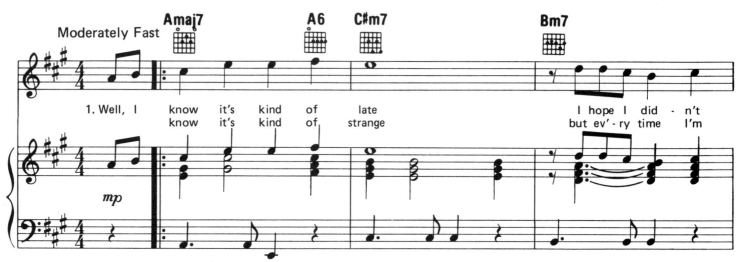

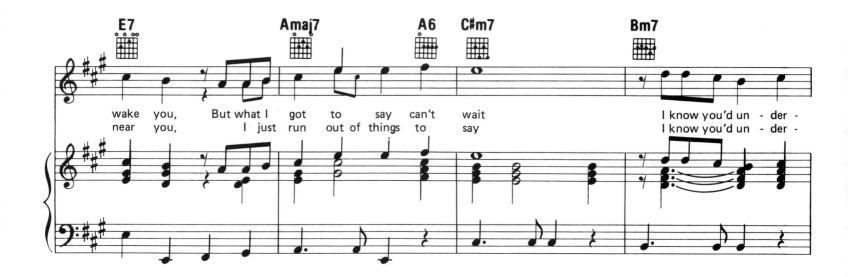

I'm Every Woman

Words and Music by
Nickolas Ashford and Valerie Simpson

I'm   ev - 'ry wom - an.   It's all ___ in ___

me. _____ An-y - thing __ you want done, ba - by,

Cm

I'll do it nat - 'ral - ly. _____

Fm9

I'm ev - 'ry wom - an. It's all __ in _____ me. _____

1.2. I can read your thoughts right now. ____ Ev - 'ry word from A ____ to Z.
3. An - y - thing you want done, ba - by, I'll do it nat - 'ral - ly.

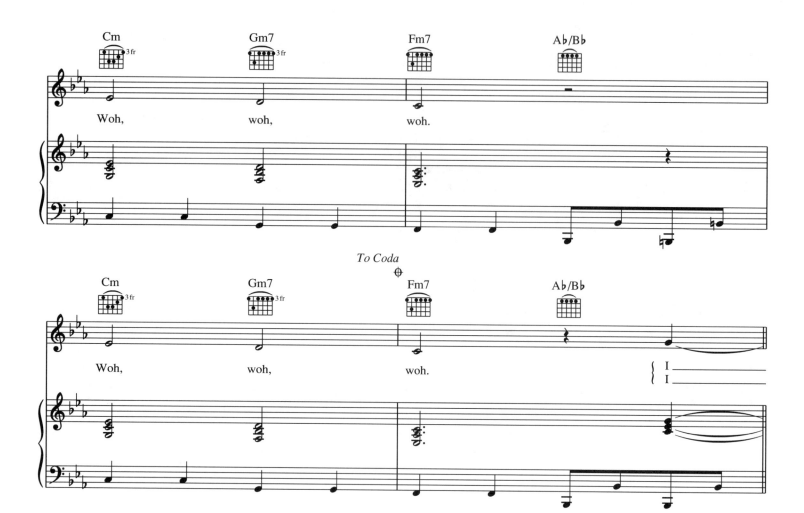

Woh,   woh,   woh.

To Coda ⊕

Woh,   woh,   woh.   I _____ I _____

__ can cast a spell _____ of se-crets you __ can't tell. _____
__ can sense your needs _____ like rain un-to __ the seeds. _____

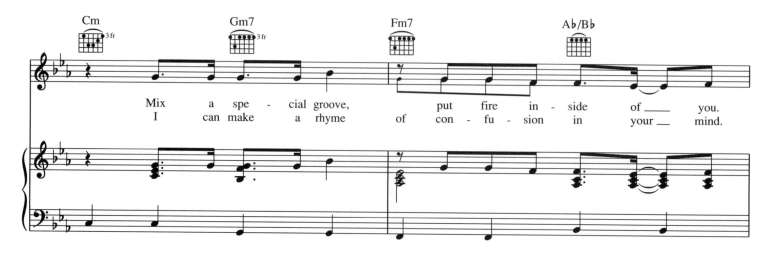

Mix a spe-cial groove,   put fire in-side of __ you.
I can make a rhyme of con-fu-sion in your __ mind.

An - y time __ you feel __ dan - ger __ or fear, __ in - stant -
And when it __ comes down __ to some good old - fash - ioned love, __ that's what

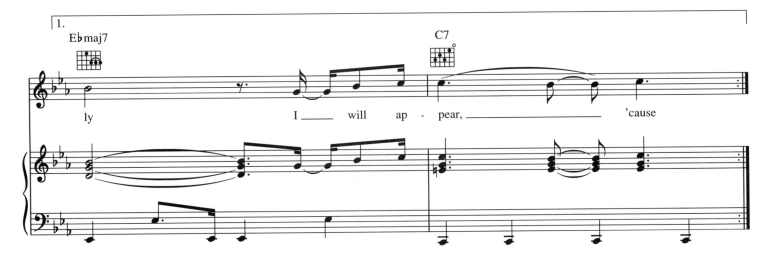

1.
ly I ____ will ap - pear, _____ 'cause

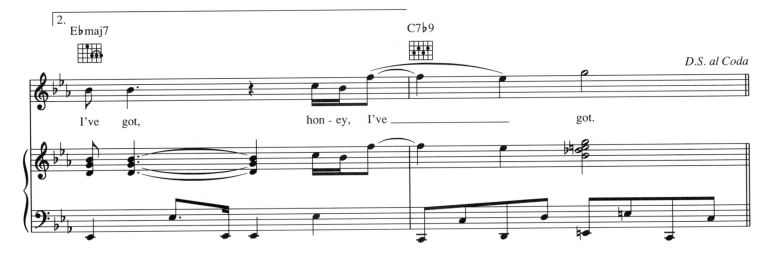

2.
D.S. al Coda

I've got, hon - ey, I've _____ got.

Coda
woh.

N.C.   N.C.

I ain't brag - gin',

'cause I'm the one. _____ You just ask me,

ooh, _____ and it shall be done. _____ And don't both - er

to ___ com - pare. ___ 'Cause I got it. _____

Cm   Gm7   **1.2.** Fm7   Ab/Bb   **3.** Fm7   Ab/Bb

Woh,   woh,   woh.   woh,

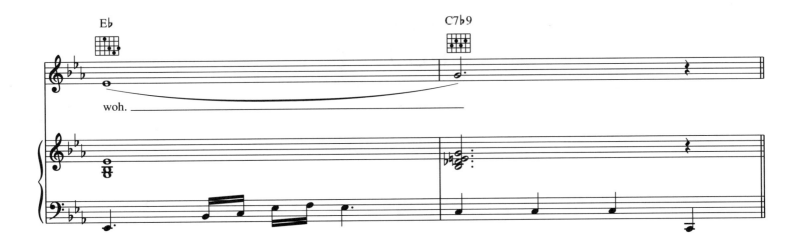

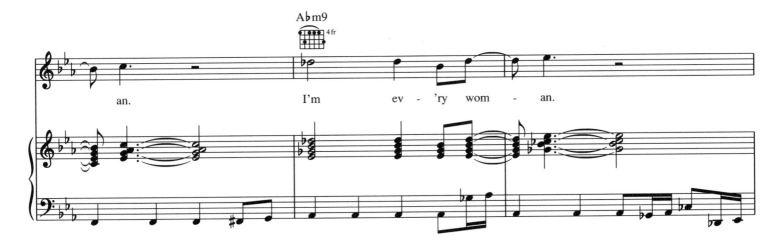

Repeat and fade

(I've Had)
The Time of My Life

from DIRTY DANCING

Words and Music by
Franke Previte, John DeNicola
and Donald Markowitz

owe it all to you. _____

Male: I've been wait-ing for so long; _____ now I've

fi-n'lly found some-one _ to stand by me.   *Female:* We saw the

writ-ing on the wall _____ as we felt this mag-i-cal _ fan-ta-

sy. _____

Both: Now   with

pas - sion in our eyes _____ there's no way we could dis - guise _____ it se - cret -

ly. _____

So we

take each oth-er's hand _____ 'cause we seem to un - der - stand _ the ur - gen -

cy.   *Male:* Just _ re - mem - ber,   *Female:* you're the

one thing   *Male:* I can't get e - nough _ of.   *Female:* So I'll tell you

some - thing: *Both:* this could be love.   Be - cause   I've _ had _

_ the time of my life. ___   No, I nev - er felt _ this way be -

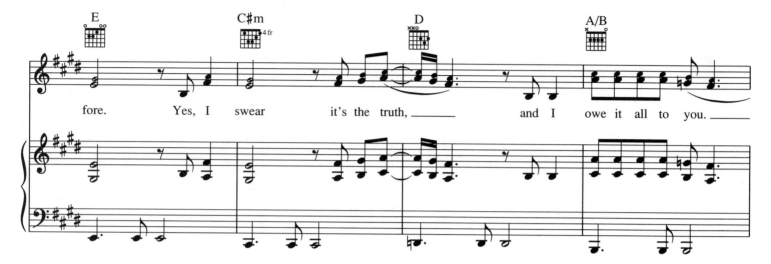

fore.   Yes, I swear   it's the truth, _____   and I   owe it all to you. _____

Male: Hey,   ba - by.

Female: With   my   bod - y   and soul, _____   I want   you

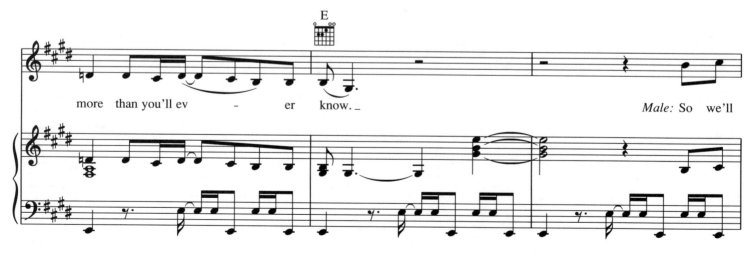

more than you'll ev - er   know. _

Male: So we'll

just let it go; _ don't be a-fraid to lose con-trol. ___

Female: Yes, I know what's on _ your mind when you say stay with me to-

night. _____ *Male:* Stay _ with me. Just re-mem-ber, you're the

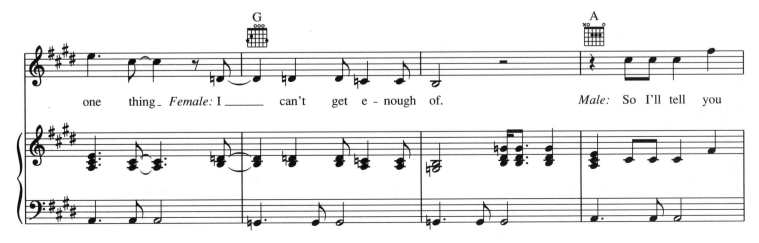

one thing _ *Female:* I _____ can't get e-nough of. *Male:* So I'll tell you

some - thing: __ *Both:* this could be love. Be - cause I've __ had __
I've

__ the time of my life. __ No, I nev - er felt __ this way be -
had the time of my life. __ And I've searched through ev - 'ry o - pen

fore. Yes, I swear it's the truth, _____ and I
door till I've found the __ truth, _____ and I

owe it all to you. __ 'Cause __ owe it all to you. _____

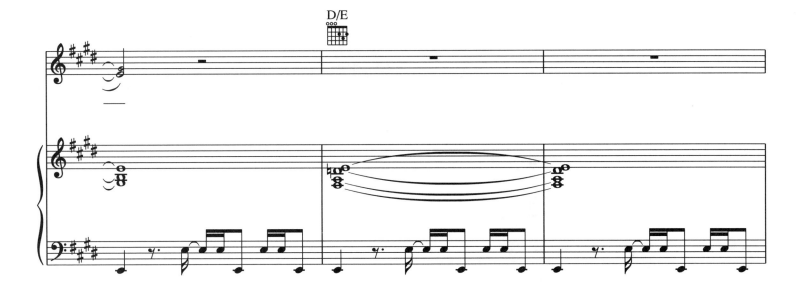

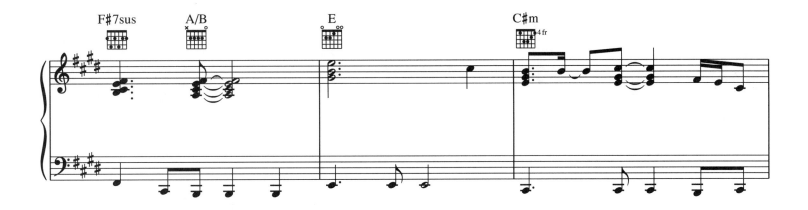

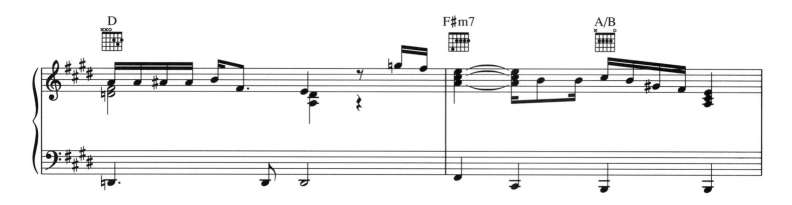

N.C.

Male: Now

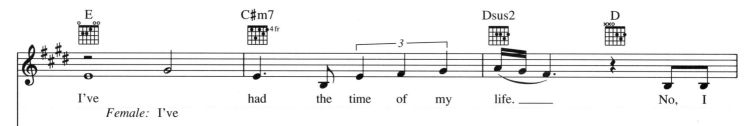

E   C#m7   Dsus2   D

I've   had   the   time   of my   life. _____   No, I

Female: I've

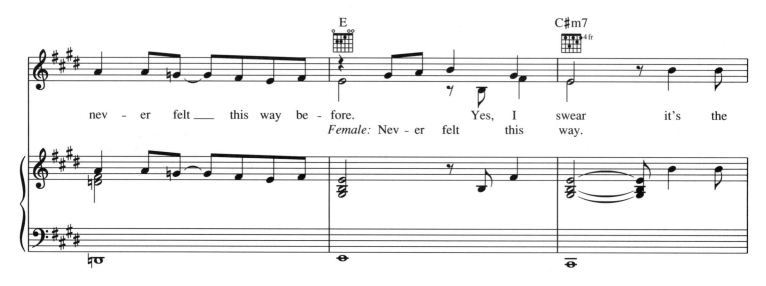

E   C#m7

nev - er   felt ___ this way be - fore.   Yes, I   swear   it's the

Female: Nev - er felt   this   way.

If

Words and Music by
David Gates

Moderately, with feeling

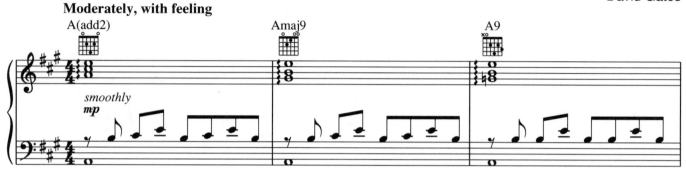

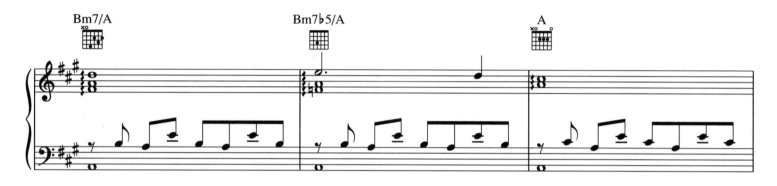

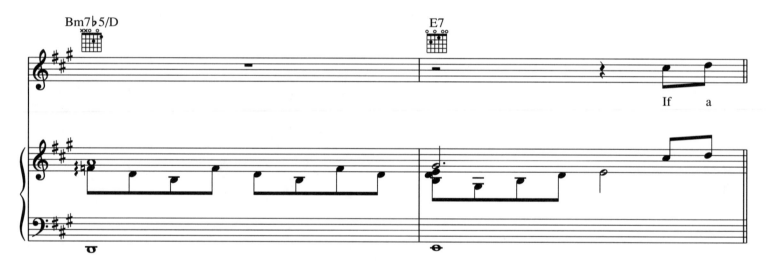

If a

pic - ture paints a thou - sand words, ___ then why ___
man could be a two plac - es at ___ one time, ___

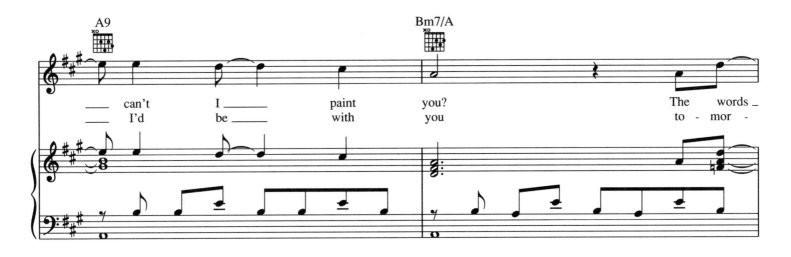

_can't I ___ paint you? The words ___
I'd be ___ with you to - mor -

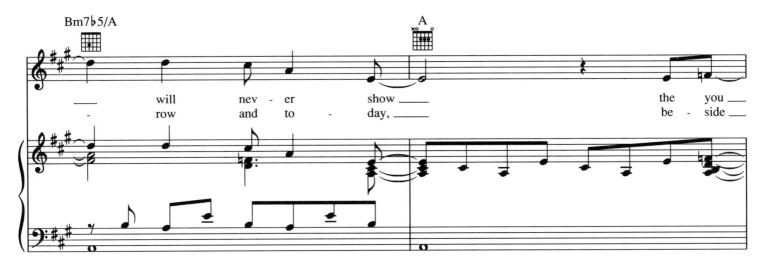

_ will nev - er show ___ the you ___
- row and to - day, ___ be - side ___

_ I've come ___ to know. ___ If a
_ you all ___ the way. ___ If the

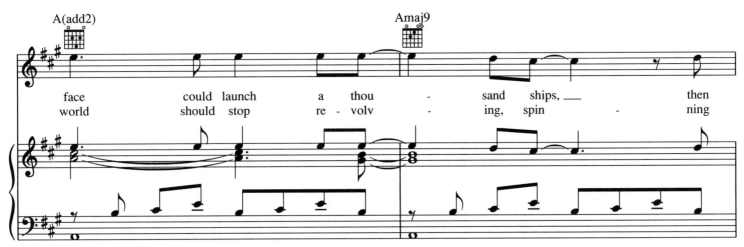

face could launch a thou - sand ships, ___ then
world should stop re - volv - ing, spin - ning

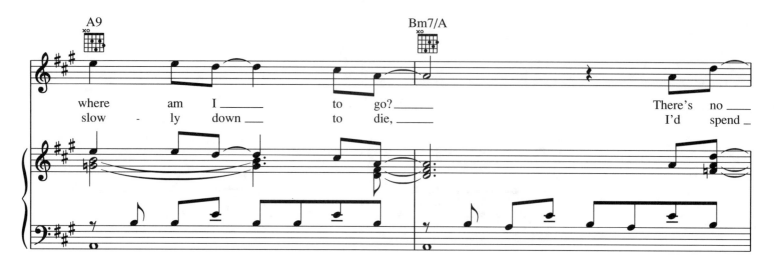

where am I _____ to go? _____ There's no _____
slow - ly down _____ to die, _____ I'd spend _____

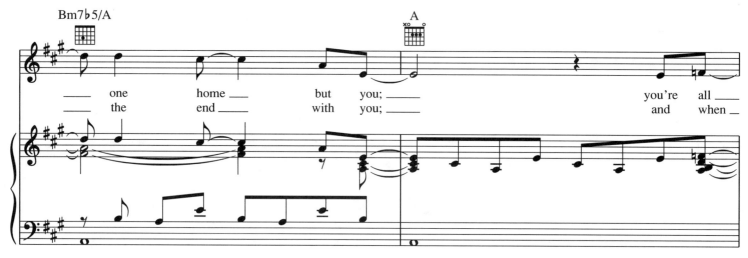

_____ one home _____ but you; _____ you're all _____
_____ the end _____ with you; _____ and when _____

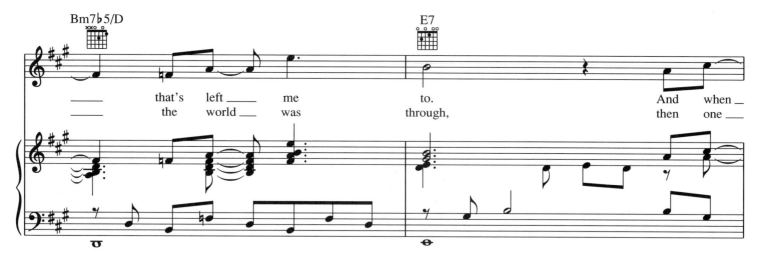

_____ that's left _____ me to. And when _____
_____ the world _____ me was through, then one _____

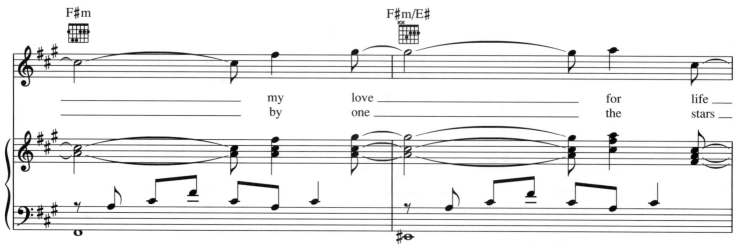

_____ my love _____ for life _____
_____ by one _____ the stars _____

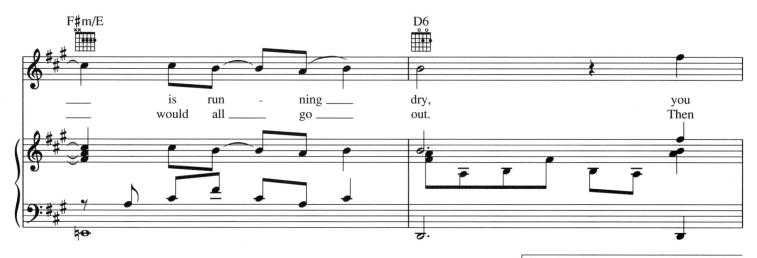

F#m/E   D6

___ is run - ning ___ dry,   you
___ would all ___ go ___ out.   Then

C#m7b5   F#m7   1. Bm7

come   and pour ___ your - self   on
you   and I ___ would

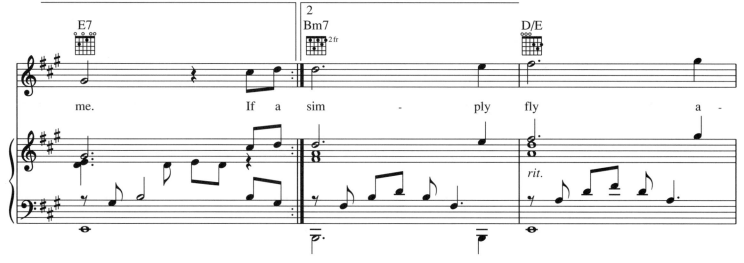

E7   2. Bm7   D/E

me.   If a sim - ply fly   a -

rit.

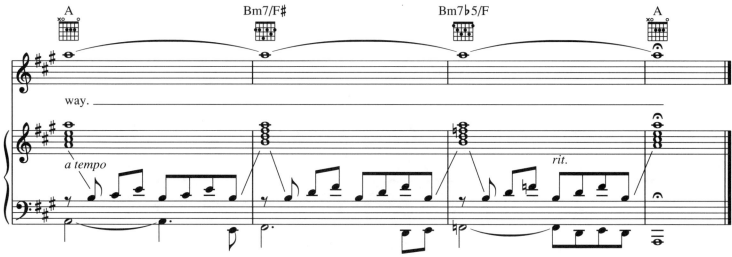

A   Bm7/F#   Bm7b5/F   A

way. ___

a tempo   *rit.*

Imagine

Words and Music by
John Lennon

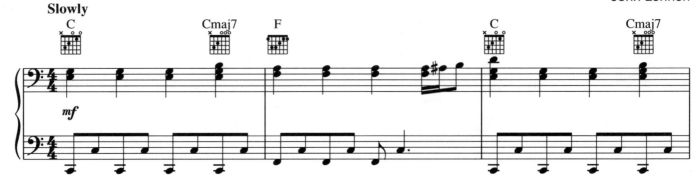

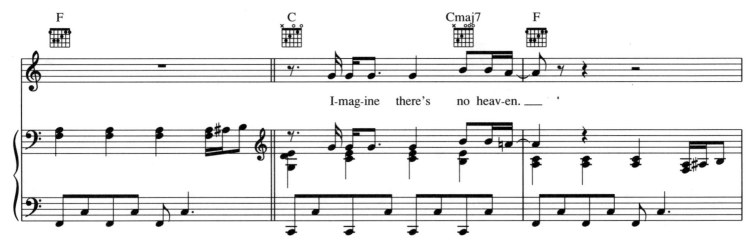

I-mag-ine there's no heav-en. __

It's eas-y if you __ try. ____ No hell __ be-low us, __

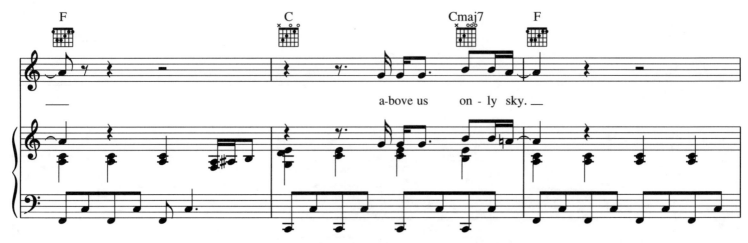

__ a-bove us on-ly sky. __

I-mag-ine all __ the peo - ple ___ liv - ing for to - day. _

___ Ah. _____ I-mag-ine there's no coun - tries.
sions.

It is - n't hard ____ to do. _____
I won-der if you ___ can. _____

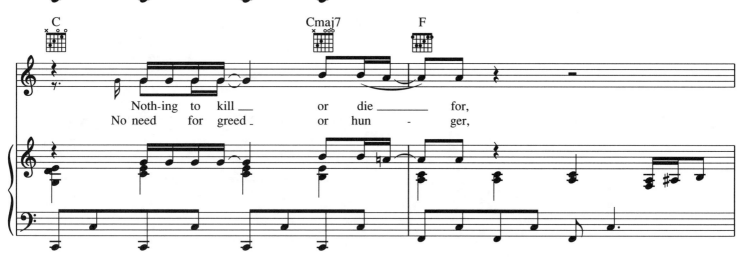

Noth-ing to kill __ or die _____ for,
No need for greed _ or hun - ger,

and no re - li - gion, ___ too. ___
a broth - er - hood ___ of man. ___

I - mag - ine all the peo - ple ___ liv - ing life in peace. ___
I - mag - ine all the peo - ple ___ shar - ing all the world. ___

You, ___ you may say ___ I'm a

dream - er, but I'm not the on - ly one. ___

In My Life

Words and Music by
John Lennon and Paul McCartney

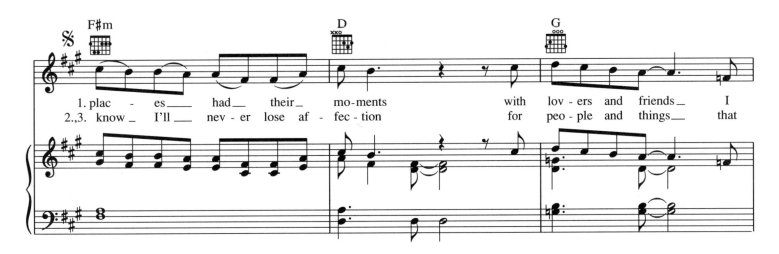

1. plac - es__ had__ their_ mo-ments with lov - ers and friends_ I
2.,3. know_ I'll _ nev - er lose af - fec - tion for peo - ple and things_ that

still can re - call. ____ Some are dead __ and__ some_ are __
went __ be - fore, __ I know I'll of - ten stop and think a -

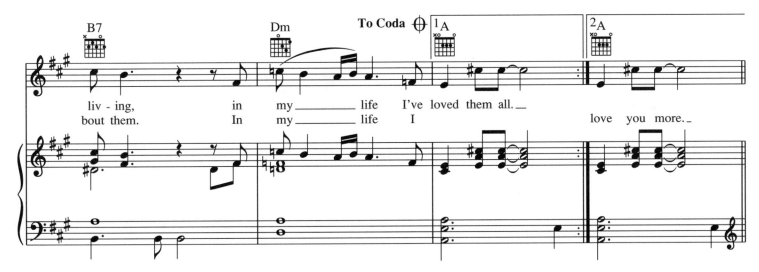

liv - ing, in my_____ life I've loved them all._
bout them. In my_____ life I love you more._

in 18th century style

143

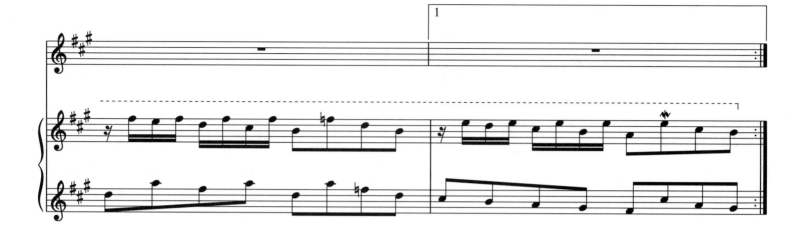

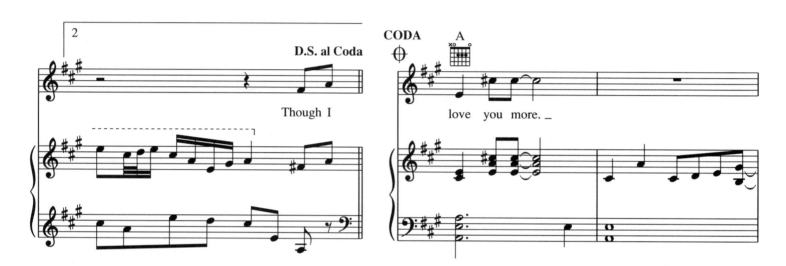

D.S. al Coda

CODA

Though I

love you more. _

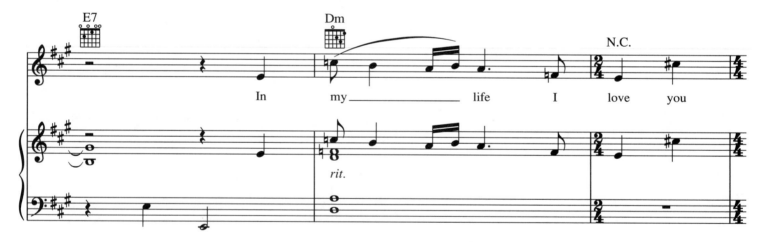

In my _____ life I love you

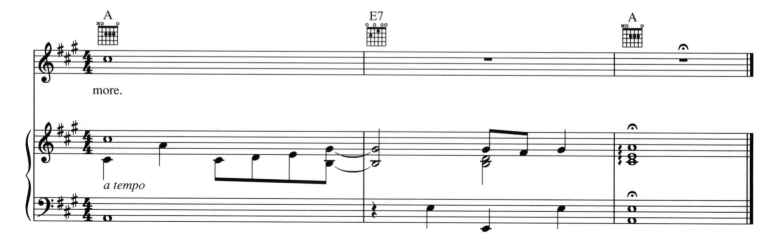

more.

Jack and Diane

Words and Music by
John Mellencamp

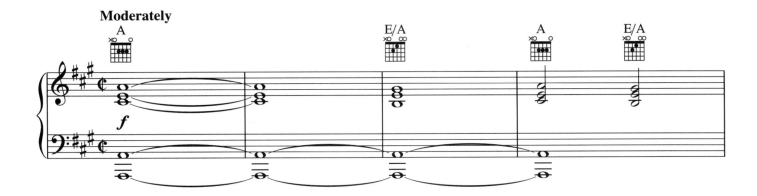

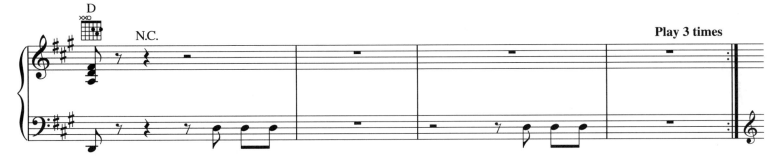

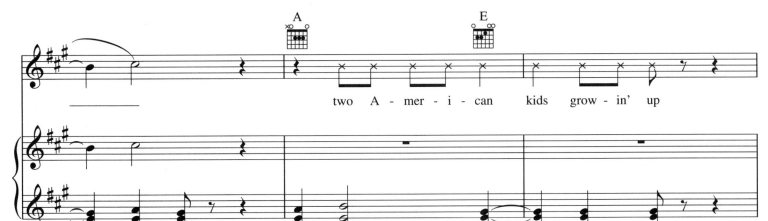

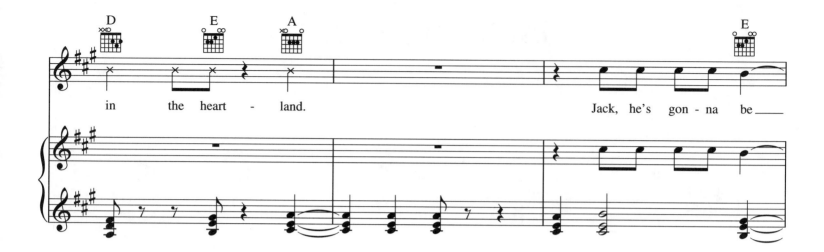

in the heart - land.   Jack, he's gon - na be ____

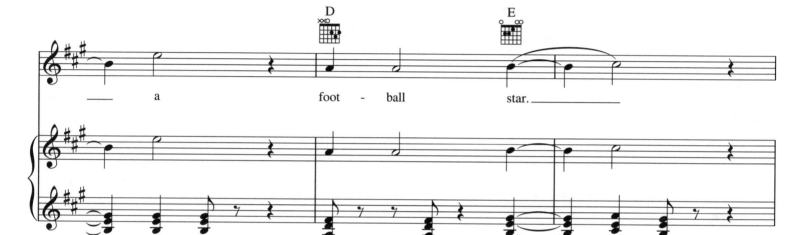

____ a   foot - ball   star. _____

Di - ane's deb - u - tante back seat   of Jack - y's car.

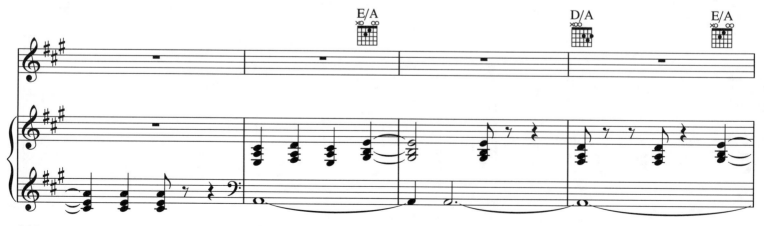

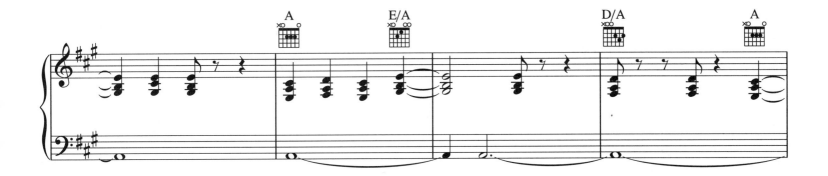

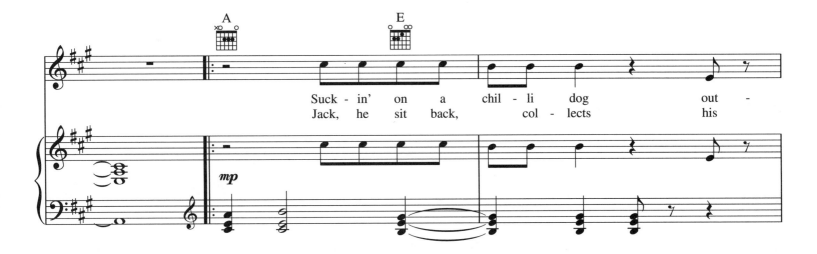

Suck - in' on a chil - li dog out -
Jack, he sit back, col - lects his

side the Tast - ee Freez;_____
thoughts for a ___ mo - ment;

Di - ane sit - tin' on
Scratch - es his

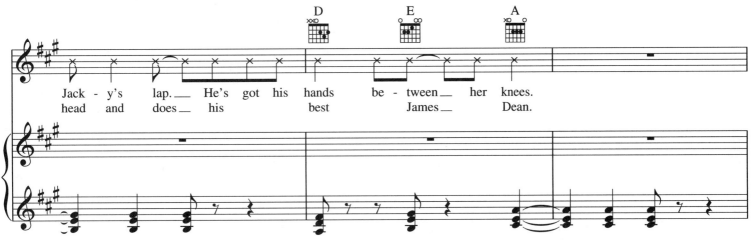

Jack - y's lap.___ He's got his hands be - tween___ her knees.
head and does___ his best James___ Dean.

Jack, he says, "Hey, Di - ane, let's run off be - hind a shad - y tree; ___
"Well, then, there, Di - ane, we got - ta run off to ___ the cit -

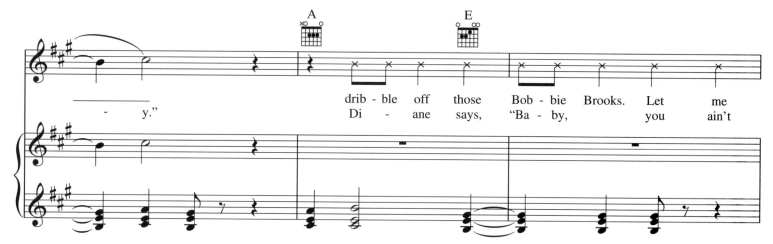

___ y."
drib - ble off those Bob - bie Brooks. Let me
Di - ane says, "Ba - by, you ain't

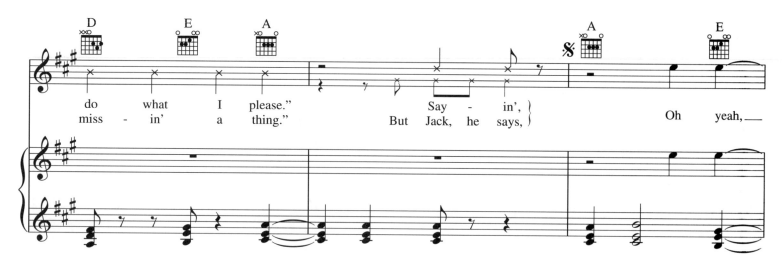

do what I please."
miss - in' a thing." But Jack, he says, Say - in', Oh yeah, ___

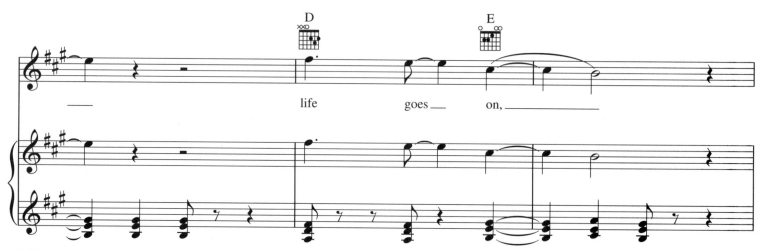

life goes ___ on, ___

148

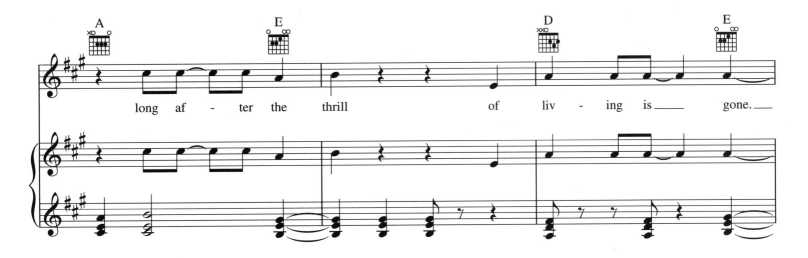

long af - ter the thrill of liv - ing is ___ gone. ___

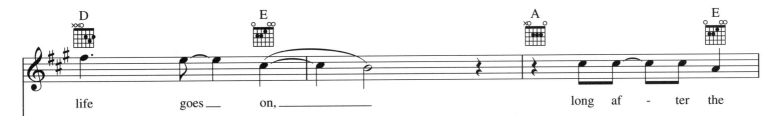

Say - in', Oh yeah, ___

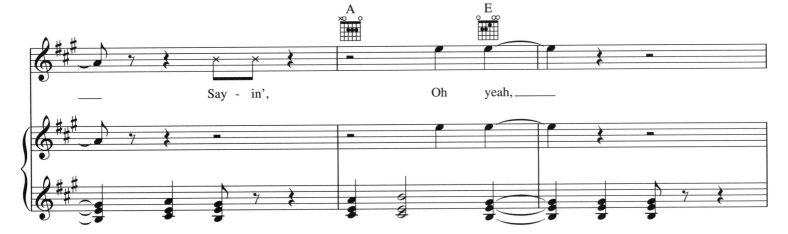

life goes ___ on, ___ long af - ter the

To Coda ⊕

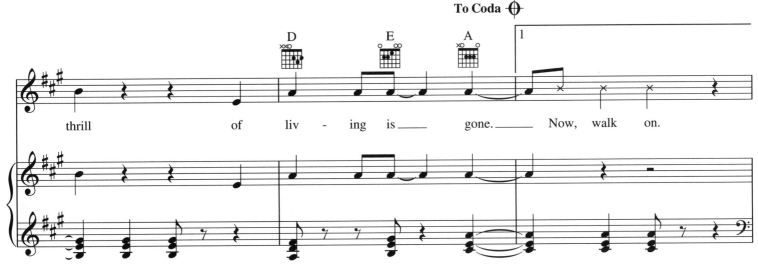

thrill of liv - ing is ___ gone. ___ Now, walk on.

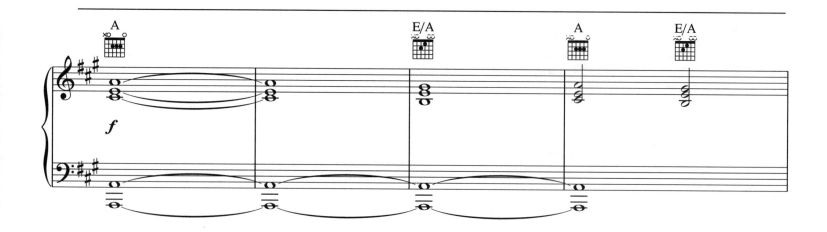

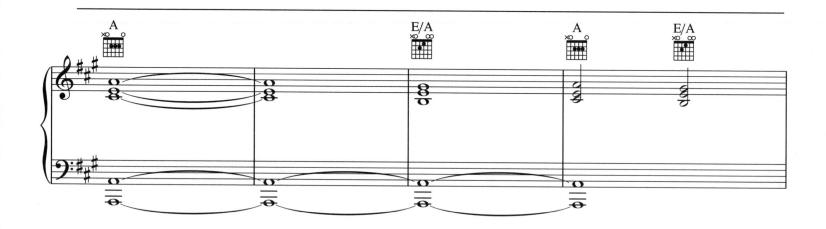

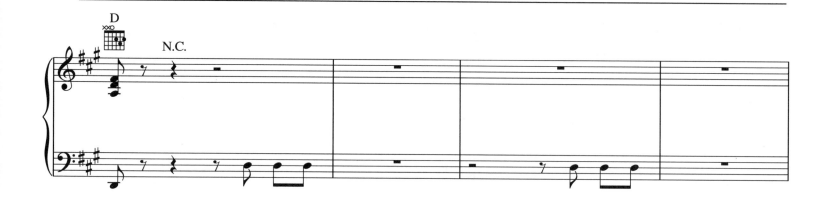

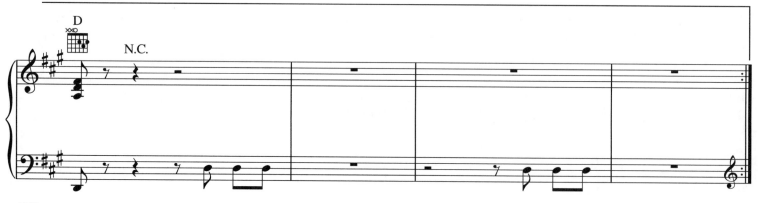

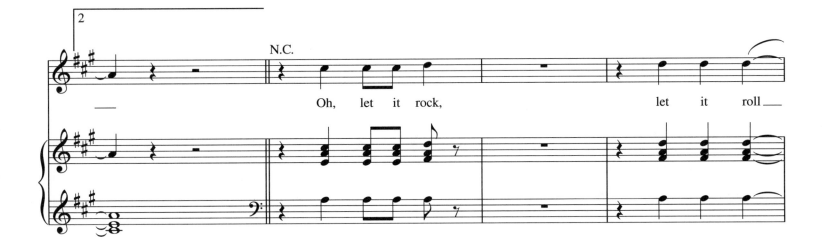

Oh, let it rock, let it roll

let the Bi - ble Belt come and

save my soul. _____ Hold - in' on to

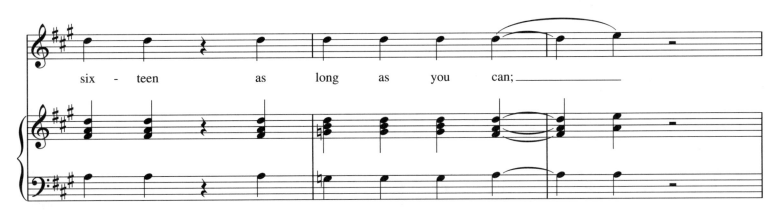

six - teen as long as you can; _____

change is com - in' 'round real soon, make us wom - en and men.

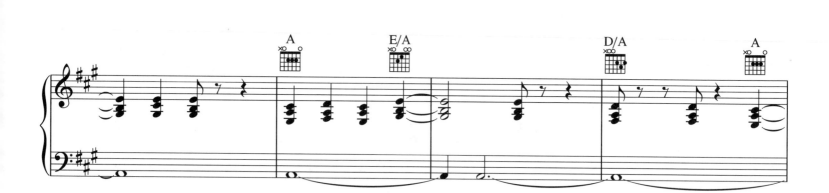

D.S. al Coda

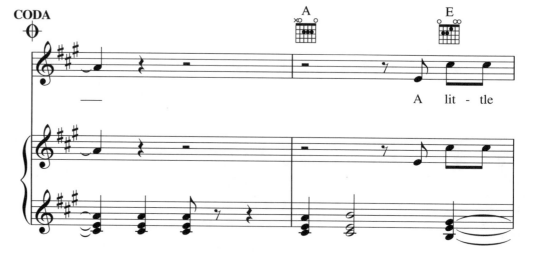

CODA

A lit - tle

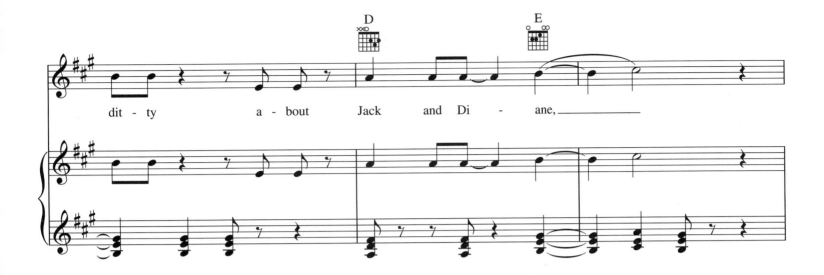

dit - ty   a - bout   Jack   and   Di - ane, _____

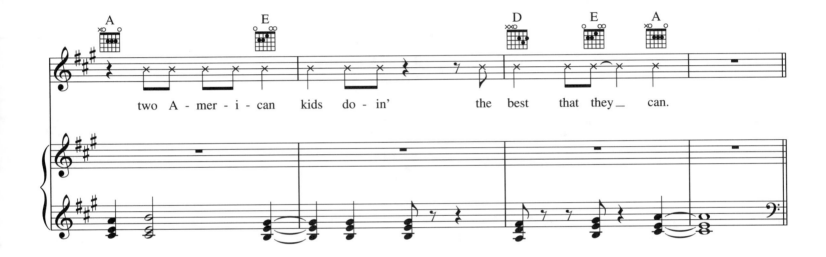

two A - mer - i - can   kids   do - in'   the   best   that   they __ can.

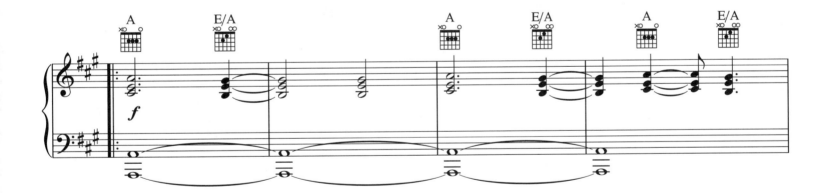

Repeat and Fade

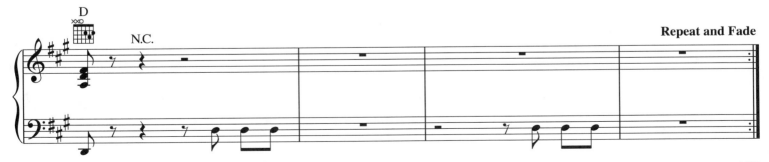

N.C.

153

Joy to the World

Words and Music by
Hoyt Axton

world. All ____ the boys and girls ___ now. Joy to the fish - es in the

deep blue sea, ___ Joy to ___ you and me. ___

You

155

Repeat and Fade

156

Lady Marmalade

Words and Music by
Bob Crewe and Kenny Nolan

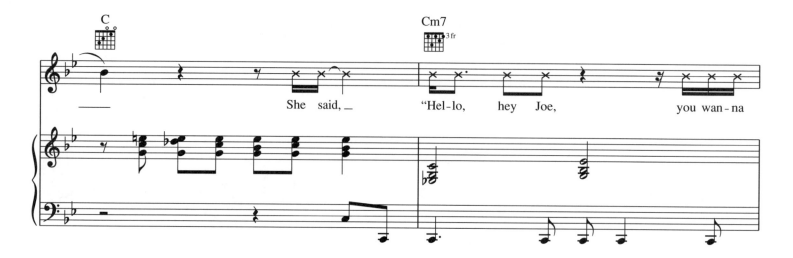

She said, — "Hel-lo, hey Joe, you wan-na

give it a go?" — Mm hmm. Get-cha get-cha ya ya da —

— da. Get - cha get - cha ya ya here. —

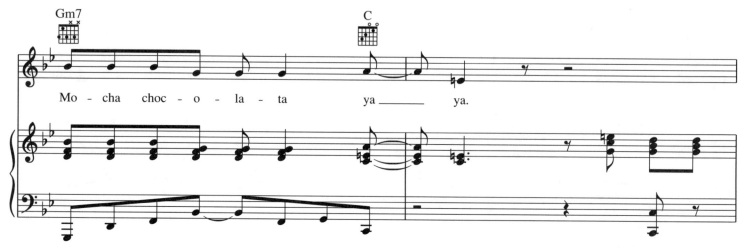

Mo - cha choc - o - la - ta ya — ya.

Cre - ole La - dy Mar - ma - lade. ___

Vou - lez vous cou - cher a - vec moi ___ ce soir? Vou - lez vous cou - cher a - vec moi? ___

Stayed in her bou - doir while she ___ fresh - ened up; ___
(Hey sis - ter, go sis - ter, soul sis - ter, go sis - ter.

that boy drank all that mag - no - lia wine. On her
Hey sis - ter, go sis - ter, soul sis - ter, go sis - ter.)

black sat - in sheets, I swear ___ he start-ed to freak. ___

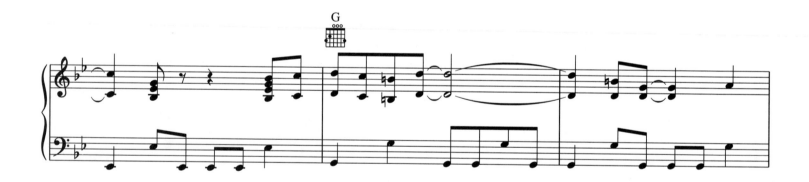

Hey, ___ hey, ___ hey ___

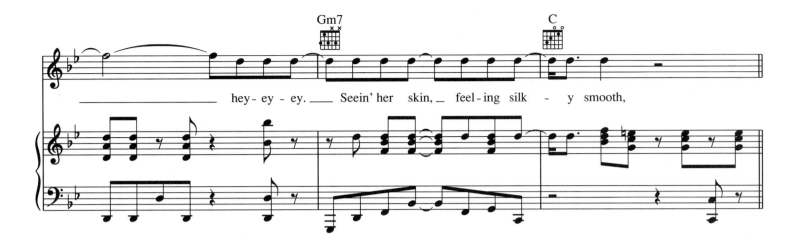

hey- ey - ey. ___ Seein' her skin, ___ feel-ing silk - y smooth,

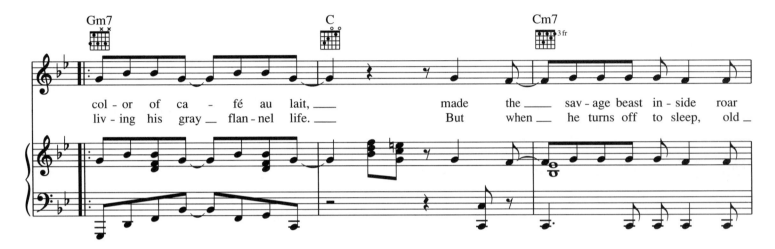

col - or of ca - fé au lait, ___ made the ___ sav - age beast in - side roar
liv - ing his gray ___ flan - nel life. ___ But when ___ he turns off to sleep, old ___

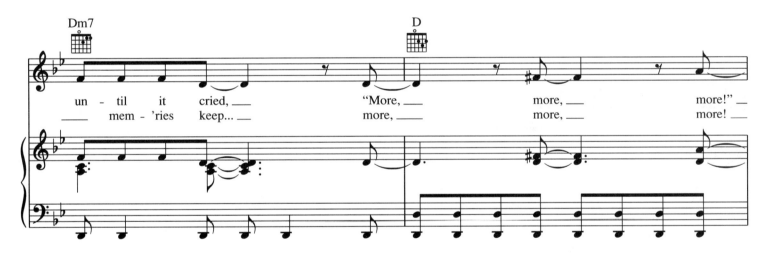

un - til it cried, ___ "More, ___ more, ___ more!" ___
___ mem - 'ries keep... ___ more, ___ more, ___ more! ___

Now he's at home ___ do - ing nine - to - five,

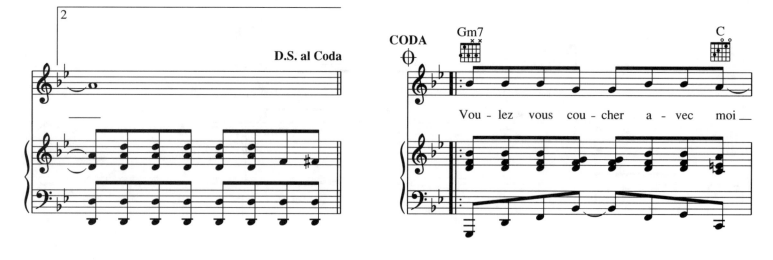

D.S. al Coda

CODA

Vou - lez vous cou - cher a - vec moi

ce soir? Vou - lez vous cou - cher a - vec moi?

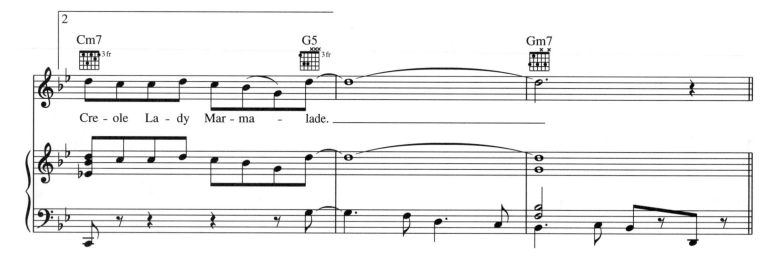

Cre - ole La - dy Mar - ma - lade.

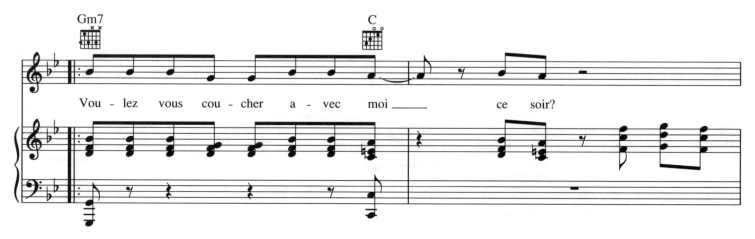

Vou - lez vous cou - cher a - vec moi ce soir?

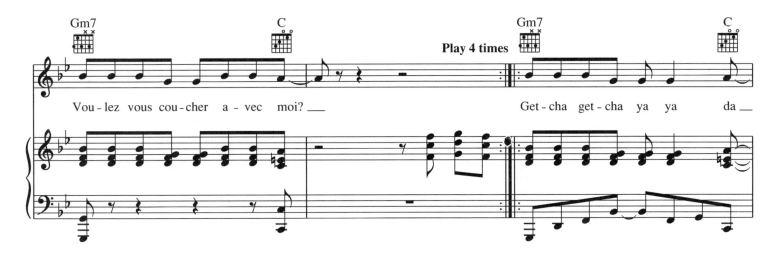

Vou- lez vous cou- cher a- vec moi? ___ Get- cha get- cha ya ya da ___

Play 4 times

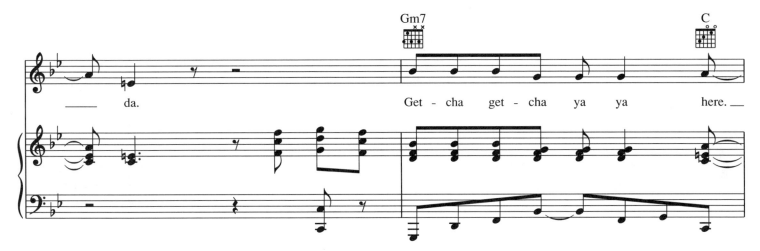

___ da. Get- cha get- cha ya ya here. ___

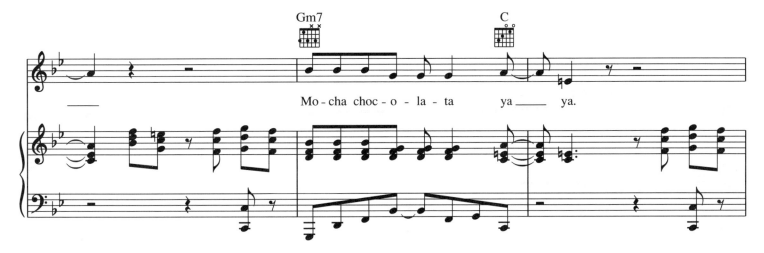

___ Mo- cha choc- o- la- ta ya ___ ya.

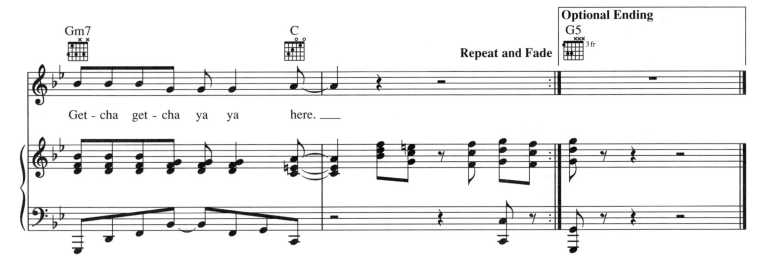

Get- cha get- cha ya ya here. ___

Repeat and Fade

Optional Ending

163

Lady in Red

Words and Music by
Chris DeBurgh

Limbo Rock

Words and Music by
Billy Strange and Jon Sheldon

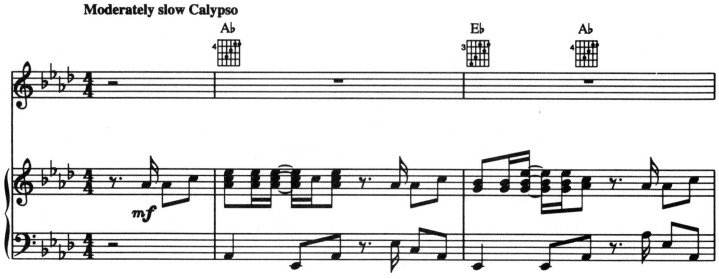

lim - bo boy _ and girl   all a - round the lim - bo world   gon - na
spread your lim - bo feet,   then you move to lim - bo beat.   Lim - bo
self a lim - bo girl,   give that chick a lim - bo whirl.   There's a

do the lim - bo rock   all a - round the lim - bo block.
an - kle, lim - bo knee,   bend back like a lim - bo tree.   Jack be
lim - bo moon a - bove,   you will fall in lim - bo love.

lim - ber, Jack be quick,   Jack go un - der lim - bo stick.   All a -

To Coda ⊕

round the lim - bo clock,   hey let's do the lim - bo rock.

(Spoken:) Limbo lower now,   *Limbo*

Percussion:

lower now.   How low can you go?   (Sung:) First, you

do the lim - bo rock.   La, la, la,   la,   la,   la,__   la, la;   la, la, la,

la,   la,   la,__   la, la;   la, la, la,   la,   la,   la,__   la, la;   la, la, la,

la,   la,   la,__   la, la;   la, la, la,   la,   la,   la,__   la, la;   la, la, la,

la, la, la, __ la, la; la, la, la, la, la, la, __ la, la; la, la, la,

la, la, la, __ la, la. Get your-

D.S. al Coda

CODA

do the lim - bo rock. no chord

(Spoken:) *Don't move that limbo bar.* *You'll be a limbo star.*

Perc.:

How low can you go? (Sung:) **La, la, la,**

la, la, la, — la, la; la, la, la, la, la, la, — la, la; la, la, la,

la, la, la, — la, la; la, la, la, la, la, la, — la, la; la, la, la,

la, la, la, — la, la; la, la, la, la, la, la, — la, la; la, la, la,

la, la, la, — la, la; la, la, la, la, la, la, — la, la.

Lowdown

Words and Music by
Boz Scaggs and David Paich

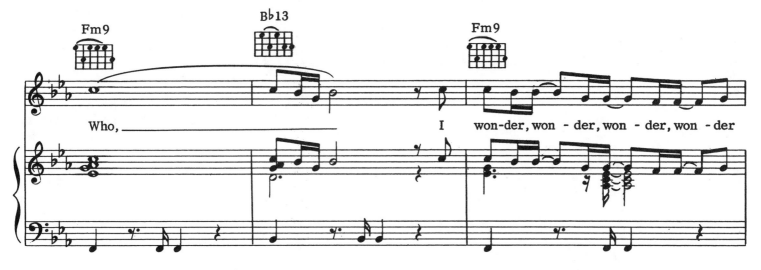

Who, _____ I won-der, won - der, won - der, won - der

who _____
{ taught her how to talk like that.
{ put those i - deas in your head.
{ got you think - in' like that, boy. }

I

1. 2.

won - der, won - der, won - der, won - der who. _____

Repeat and fade (vocal ad lib)

3.

who. _____

Repeat and fade

Love Me Tender

Words and Music by
Elvis Presley and Vera Matson

Moderately slow

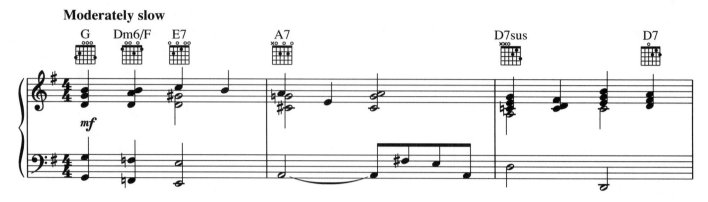

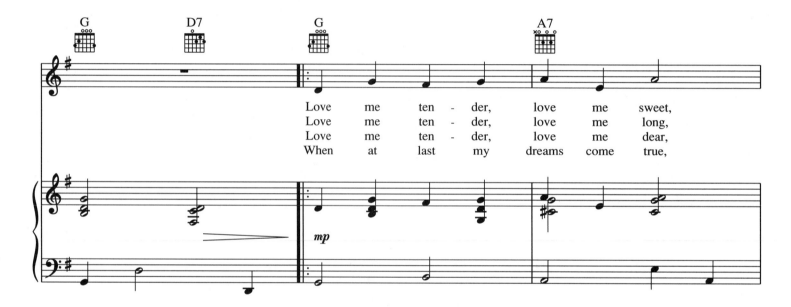

Love me ten - der, love me sweet,
Love me ten - der, love me long,
Love me ten - der, love me dear,
When at last my dreams come true,

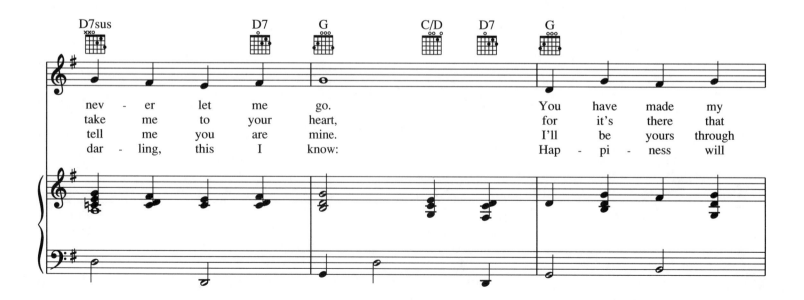

nev - er let me go.   You have made my
take me to your heart,   for it's there that
tell me you are mine.   I'll be yours through
dar - ling, this I know: Hap - pi - ness will

Magic Man

Words and Music by
Ann Wilson and Nancy Wilson

"Come on__ home,__ girl," he said with a smile.__ "I cast my spell of love__ on you: a

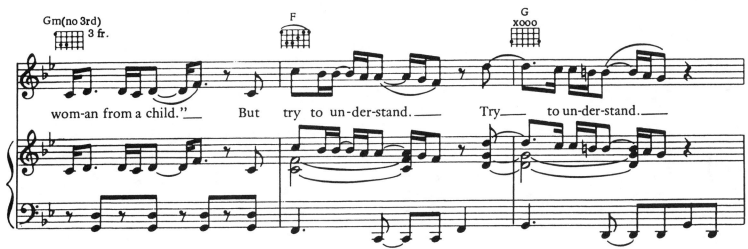

wom-an from a child." ___ But try to un-der-stand. ___ Try___ to un-der-stand. ___

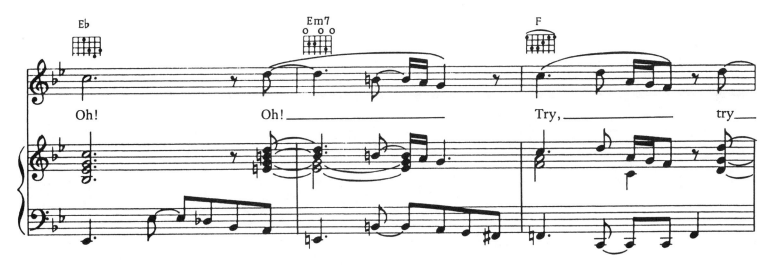

Oh! Oh! _____ Try, _____ try___

___ to un-der-stand. ___ Try, try,__ try to un-der-stand: _____ he's a mag -

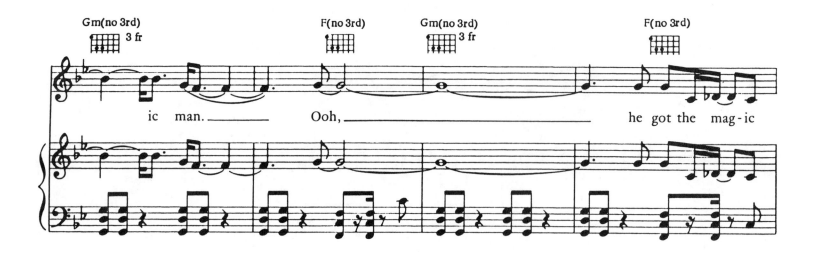

ic man._____ Ooh,_____ he got the mag-ic

hands._____

No chord

"Come on____ home,____ girl," he   said with a smile.____

"You don't have to love me yet. Let's get high a-while." But

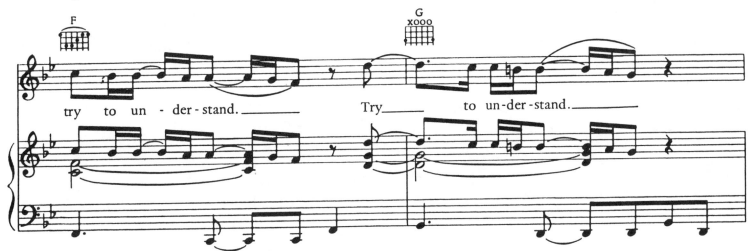

try to un-der-stand. Try to un-der-stand.

Try, try, try to un-der-stand: he's a mag-ic man.

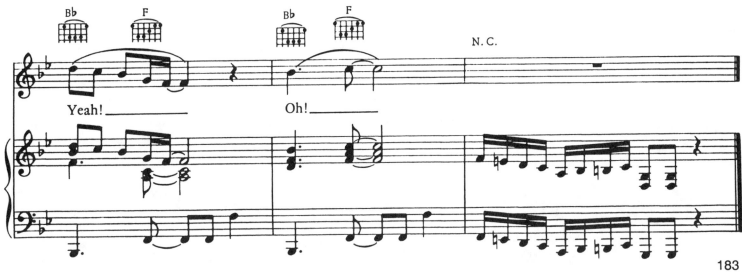

Yeah! Oh!

183

Misty Blue

Words and Music by
Bob Montgomery

Slowly

Oh, it's been such a long, long, time, Looks like I'd get you

off my mind. Oh, but I can't; just the thought of you Turns my whole world a

mist - y blue. Just a men - tion of your name Turns the flick - er

to a flame. I think of things we used to do, Then my whole world turns

mist - y blue._____ I should for - get you;

Heav - en knows_ I've tried, But when I say I'm glad we're through,

My heart knows_ I lied. Oh, it's been such a long, long time,

Oh, Pretty Woman

Words and Music by
Roy Orbison and Bill Dees

wom - an ___
wom - an ___

I don't be - lieve you, ___ you're not the
that you look love - ly ___ as can

truth
be

No one could look as good as
Are you look lone - ly just as like

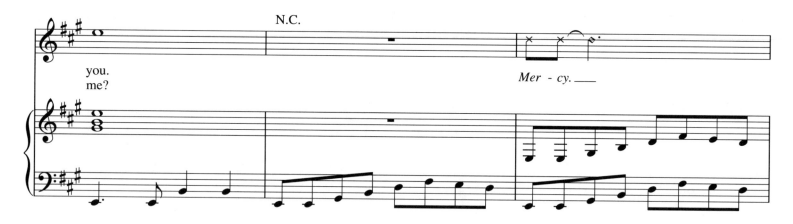

you.
me?

N.C.

Mer - cy. ___

1
E7

2
E7

Pret - ty

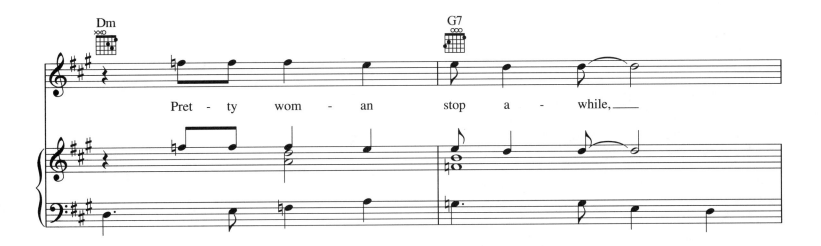

Pret - ty wom - an stop a - while,____

Pret - ty wom - an talk a - while,__ Pret - ty wom - an

give your smile__ to me.

Pret - ty wom - an yeah, yeah, yeah,_____ Pret - ty wom - an

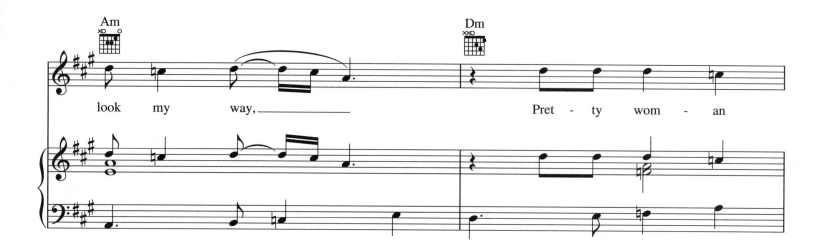

look my way,_____ Pret - ty wom - an

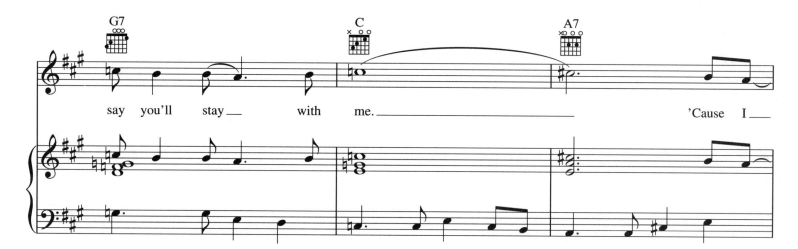

say you'll stay ___ with me._____ 'Cause I ___

___ need you ___ I'll treat you right.

Come with me ba - by. ___ Be mine to -

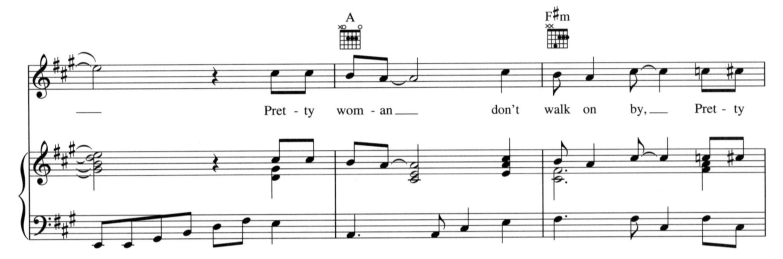

Hey,   O.   K.

If that's the way it must be___ O. K.

I guess I'll go on home,___ it's late___ There'll be to-

mor - row night but wait!   What do I see?_____

Is she walk - ing back to

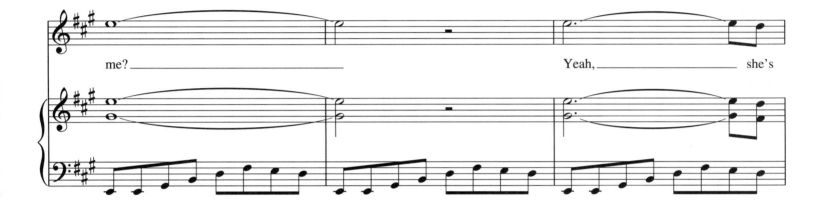

me?_____ Yeah,_____ she's

walk - ing back to me!_____

Oh,_____ Pret - ty wom - an.

Only the Lonely

Words and Music by
Martha Davis

ten - tion.
here. ___

We lied
We men - tion

a - bout each
the

oth - er's drinks; ___
time we were to - geth - er

we lived

with - out each oth - er think - ing what
so long a - go. ___ Well, I

an - y - one ___ would do ___
don't re - mem - ber. All ___ I

with - out me and you. ___
know ___ is it makes me feel ___ good now.

...Instrumental ends

1. 2. It's like I told ___ you,
3. On - ly the lone - ly,

on - ly the lone - ly can
on - ly the lone - ly can

195

The Rainbow Connection

from THE MUPPET MOVIE

Words and Music by
Paul Williams and Kenneth L. Ascher

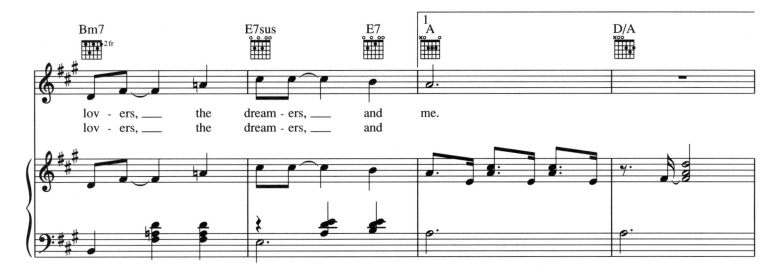

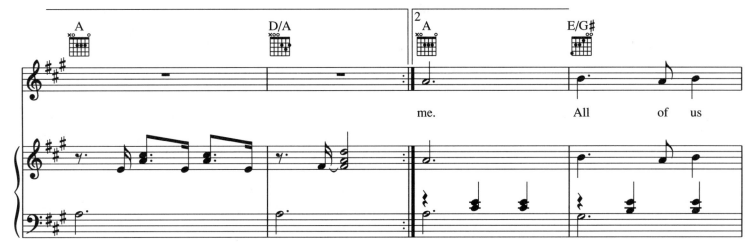

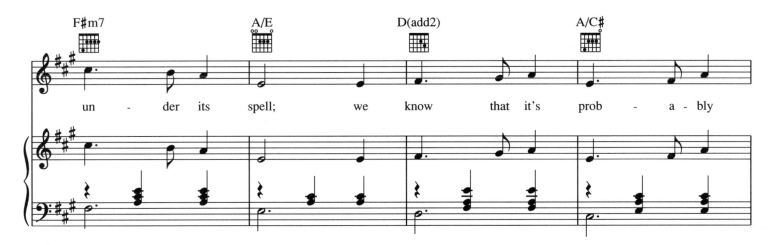

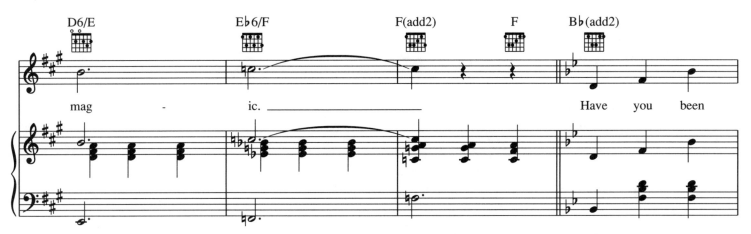

half a-sleep and have you heard voic - es? I've heard them

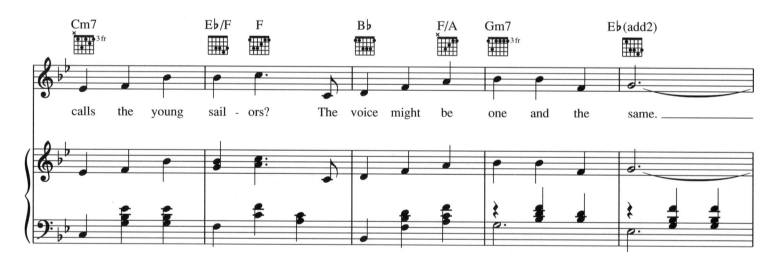

call - ing my name. _____ Is this the sweet sound _ that

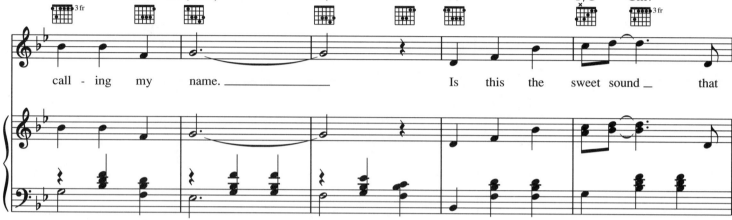

calls the young sail - ors? The voice might be one and the same. _____

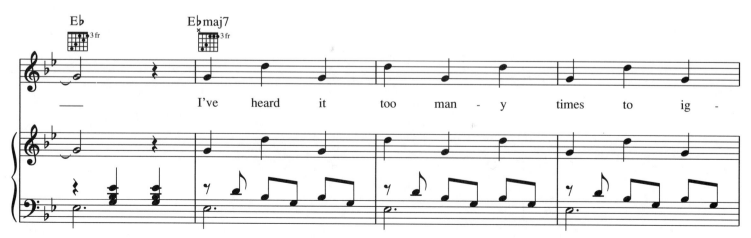

___ I've heard it too man - y times to ig -

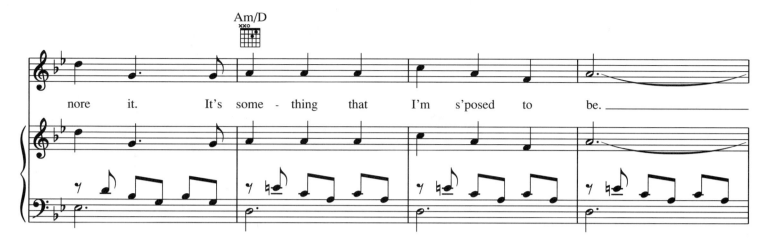

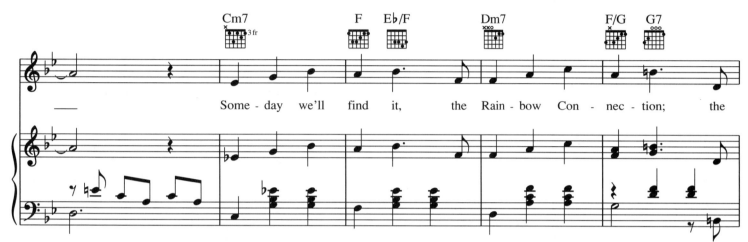

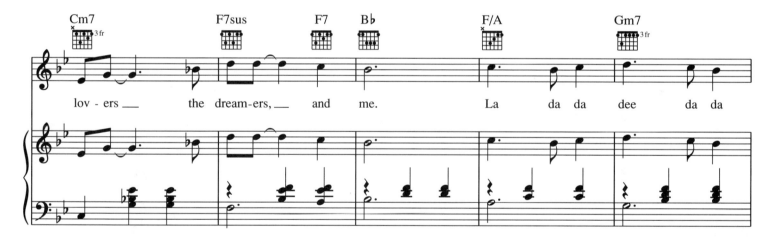

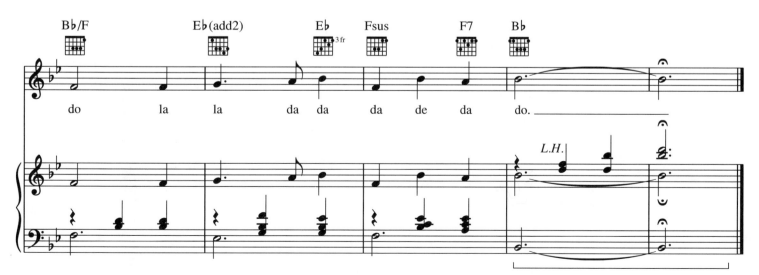

Rainy Days and Mondays

Lyrics by Paul Williams

Music by Roger Nichols

Rain - y days and Mon - days al - ways get me ___ down. ___

Fun - ny, but it seems ___ I al - ways
(D.S.) *Instrumental solo ad lib.*

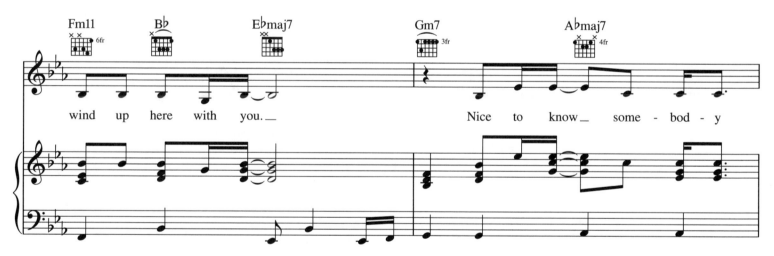

wind up here with you. ___ Nice to know ___ some - bod - y

loves ___ me.

solo ends } Fun - ny, but it seems ___ that it's ___ the

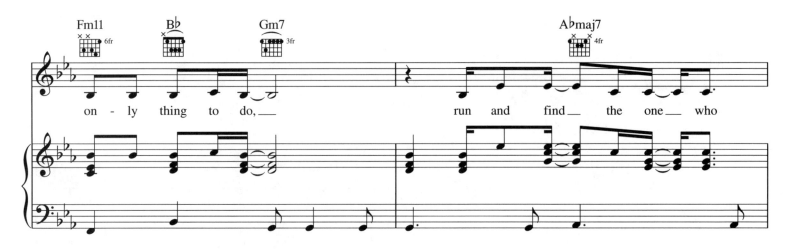

on - ly thing to do, ___ run and find ___ the one ___ who

To Coda ⊕

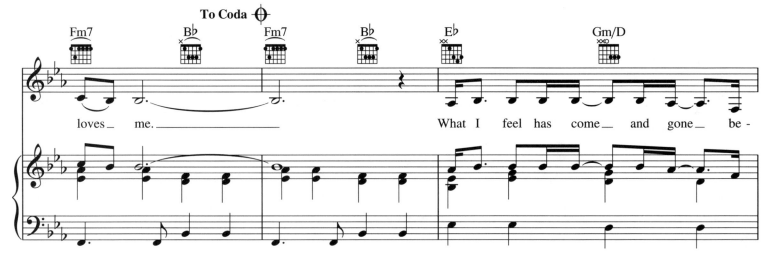

loves ___ me. _____ What I feel has come ___ and gone ___ be -

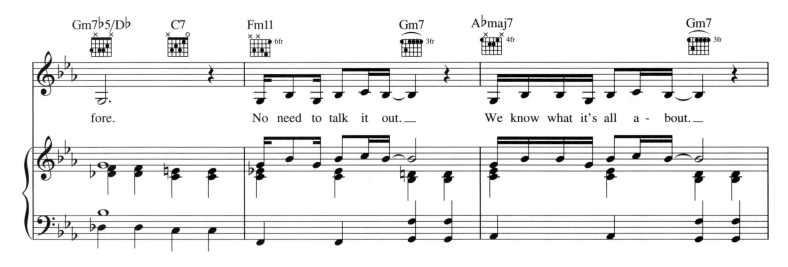

fore. No need to talk it out. ___ We know what it's all a - bout. ___

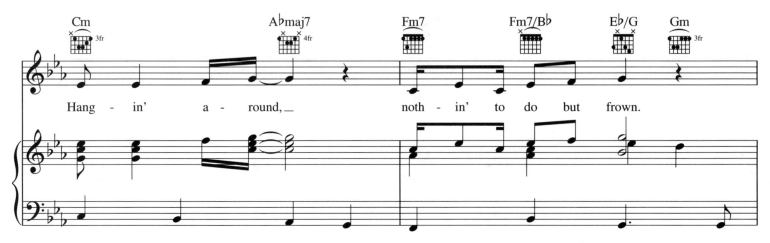

Hang - in' a - round, ___ noth - in' to do but frown.

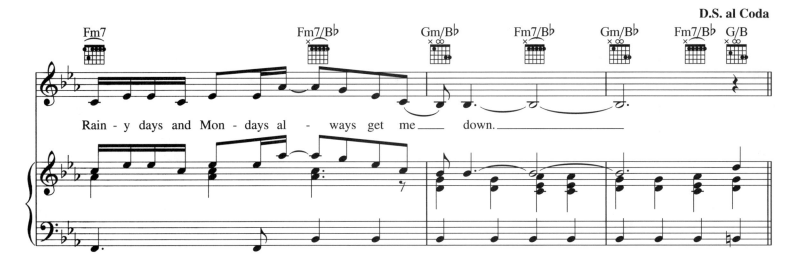

Rain - y days and Mon - days al - ways get me down.

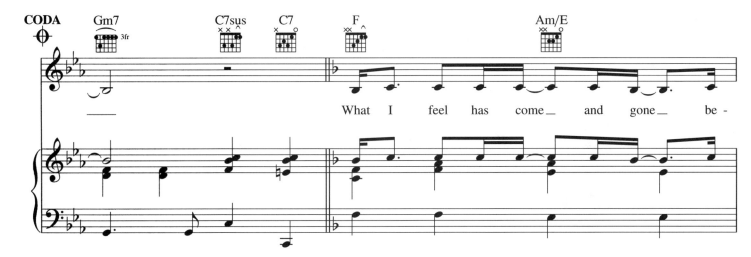

What I feel has come and gone be -

fore. No need to talk it out.

We know what it's all a - bout. Hang - in' a - round,

nothin' to do but frown. Rain-y days and Mon-days al - ways get me

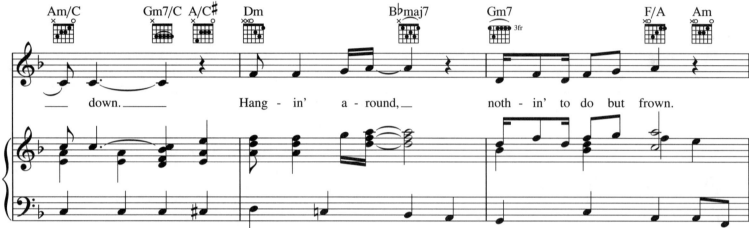

down. Hang-in' a - round, nothin' to do but frown.

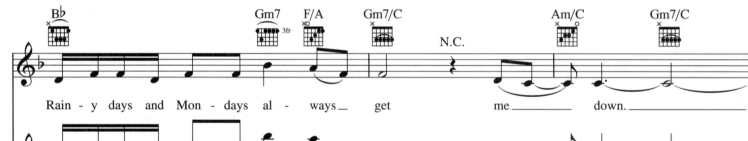

Rain-y days and Mon-days al - ways get me down.

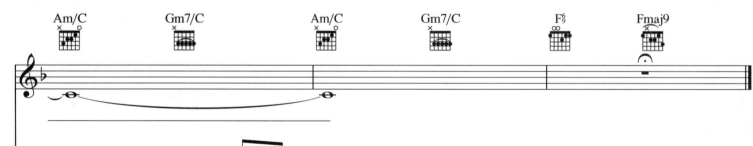

Respect

Words and Music by
Otis Redding

Solid 4 Beat

What you want ba-by I got.
I ain't gon-na do you wrong while you gone.

What you need You know I got it.
I ain't gon-na do you wrong 'Cause I don't wan-na.

All I'm ask-in'   is for a lit-tle re -spect, when you come home.   Ba-

- by,   when you come home,___   Re - spect.

I'm out___ to give you   all   my mon-ey,   But all I'm ask-in'
Ooh,___ your kiss-es,   sweeter than hon-ey,   But guess___ what,___

in re -turn,   hon - ey,   Is to give me
so here's my   mon-ey,   All I want you   to do for me

208

Repeat and fade out

209

Rock Around the Clock

Words and Music by
Max C. Freedman and Jimmy DeKnight

Rocky Mountain High

Words and Music by
John Denver and Mike Taylor

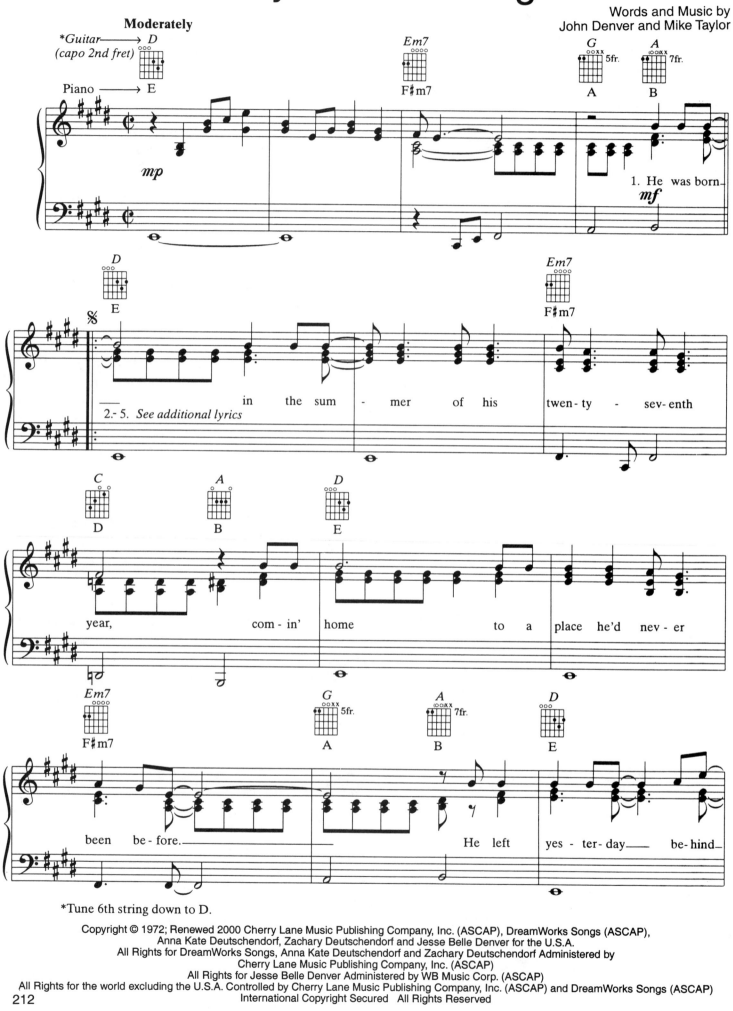

*Tune 6th string down to D.

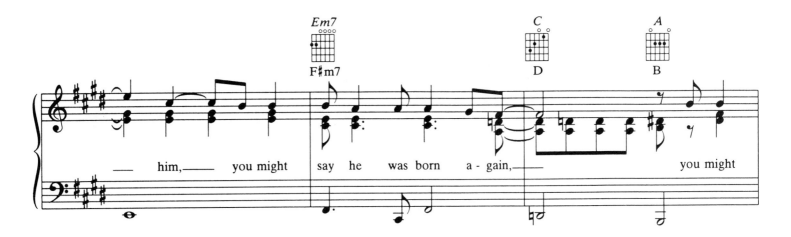

him,___ you might say he was born a-gain,___ you might

say he found___ a key___ for ev - 'ry door.___

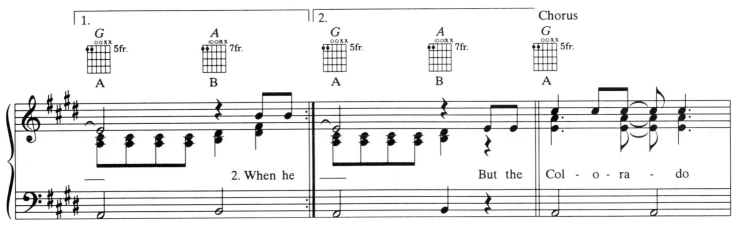

1.

2. When he

2.

Chorus

But the Col - o - ra - do

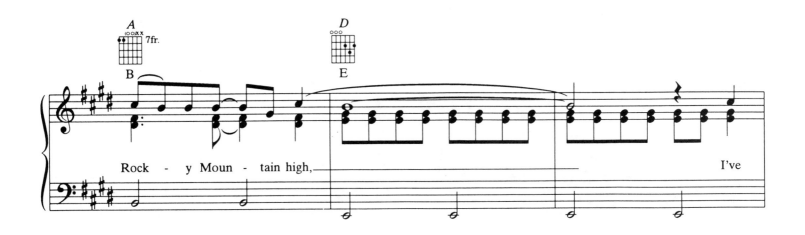

Rock - y Moun - tain high,___ I've

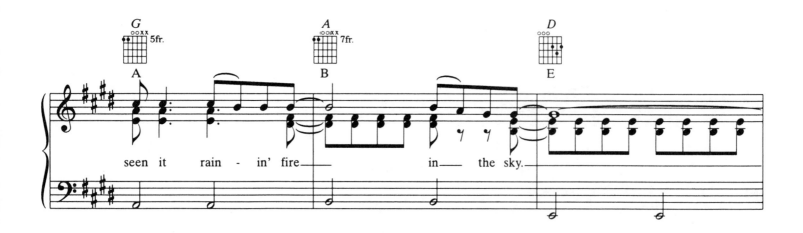

seen it rain - in' fire___ in___ the sky.___

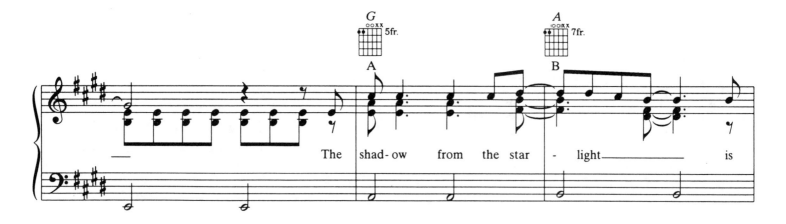

___ The shad-ow from the star - light___ is

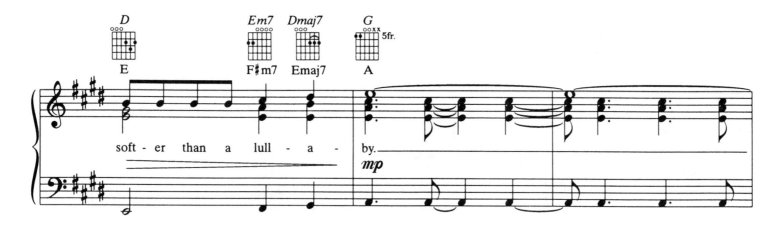

soft - er than a lull - a - by.___

mp

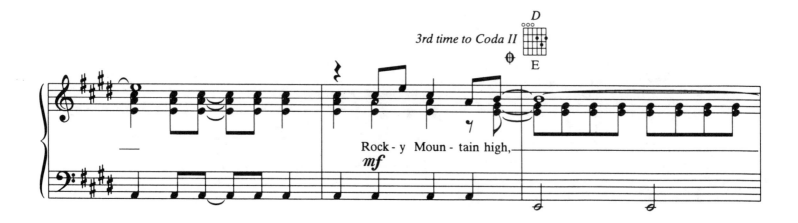

3rd time to Coda II

___ Rock - y Moun - tain high,___

mf

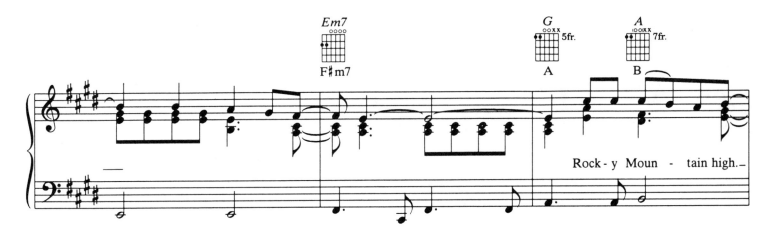

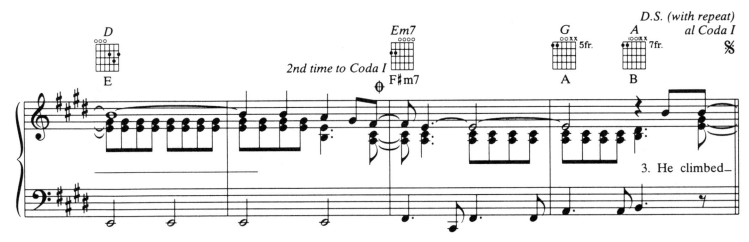

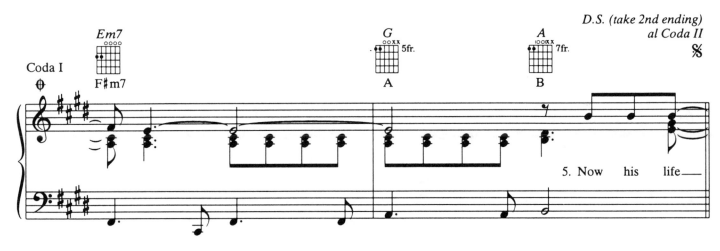

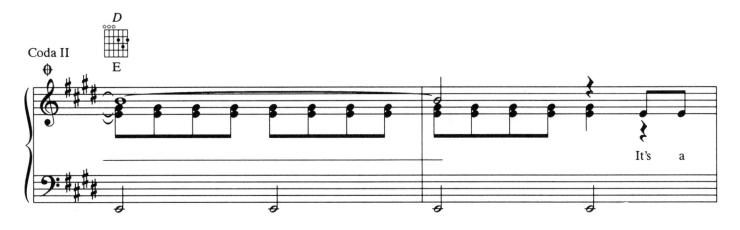

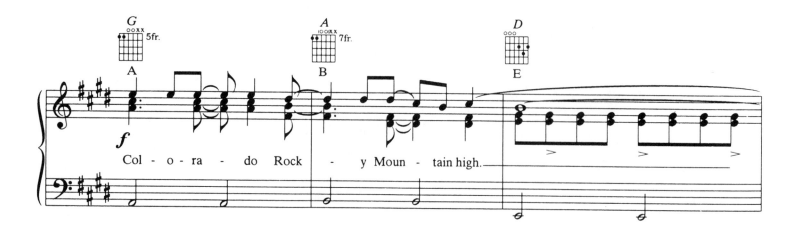

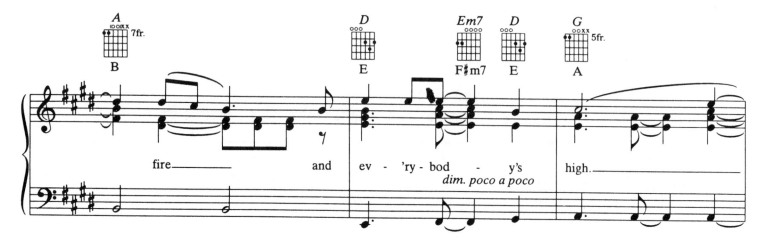

Rock - y Moun - tain high.—

mp *mf*

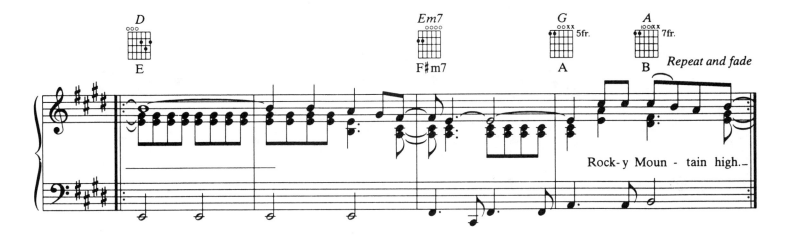

Rock - y Moun - tain high.—

Repeat and fade

Additional Lyrics

2. When he first came to the mountains his life was far away,
   On the road and hangin' by a song.
   But the string's already broken and he doesn't really care.
   It keeps changin' fast, and it don't last for long. *(To 1st Chorus)*

3. He climbed cathedral mountains, he saw silver clouds below.
   He saw everything as far as you can see.
   And they say that he got crazy once and he tried to touch the sun,
   And he lost a friend but kept his memory.

4. Now he walks in quiet solitude the forests and the streams,
   Seeking grace in every step he takes.
   His sight has turned inside himself to try and understand
   The serenity of a clear blue mountain lake.

   2nd Chorus:
   And the Colorado Rocky Mountain high,
   I've seen it rainin' fire in the sky.
   You can talk to God and listen to the casual reply.
   Rocky Mountain high.
   Rocky Mountain high.

5. Now his life is full of wonder but his heart still knows some fear
   Of a simple thing he cannot comprehend.
   Why they try to tear the mountains down to bring in a couple more,
   More people, more scars upon the land.

   3rd Chorus:
   And the Colorado Rocky Mountain high,
   I've seen it rainin' fire in the sky.
   I know he'd be a poorer man if he never saw an eagle fly.
   Rocky Mountain high.

Rosanna

Words and Music by
David Paich

(Sittin' On)
The Dock of the Bay

Words and Music by
Steve Cropper and Otis Redding

Looks like noth-in's gon-na change; ___ ev - 'ry-thing

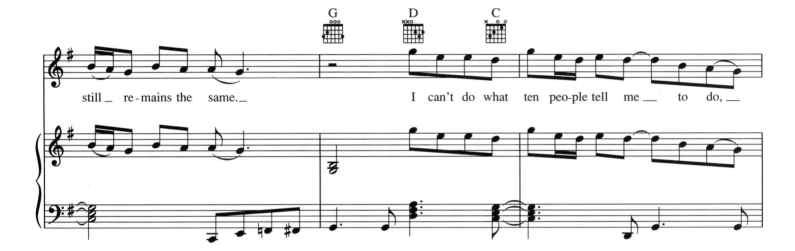

still __ re-mains the same. __ I can't do what ten peo-ple tell me __ to do, __

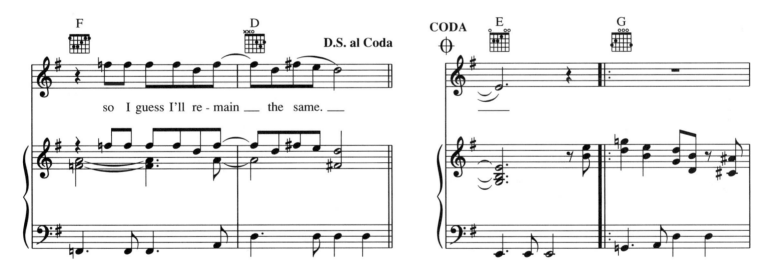

so I guess I'll re-main __ the same. __

D.S. al Coda

CODA

Repeat ad lib. | Optional Ending

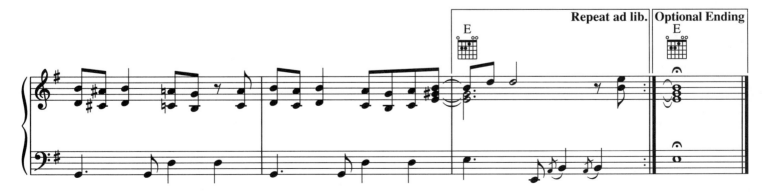

225

Shout

Words and Music by O'Kelly Isley,
Ronald Isley and Rudolph Isley

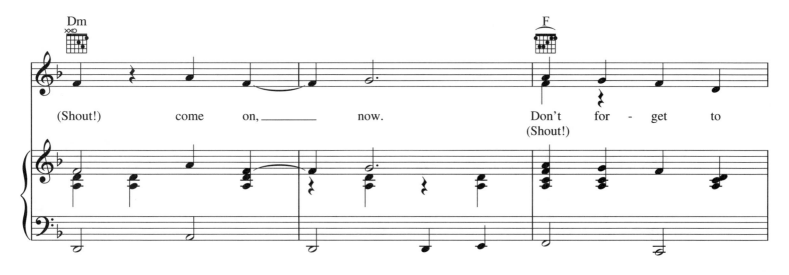

(Shout!) come on, _____ now. Don't for - get to
(Shout!)

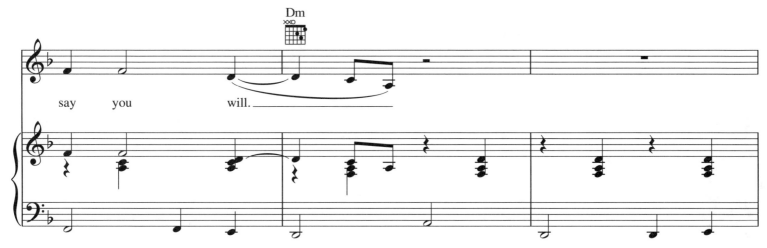

say you will. _____

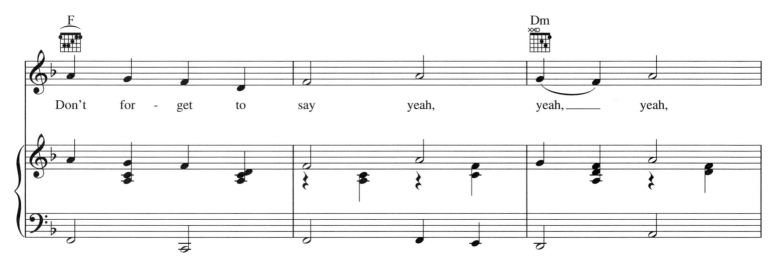

Don't for - get to say yeah, yeah, _____ yeah,

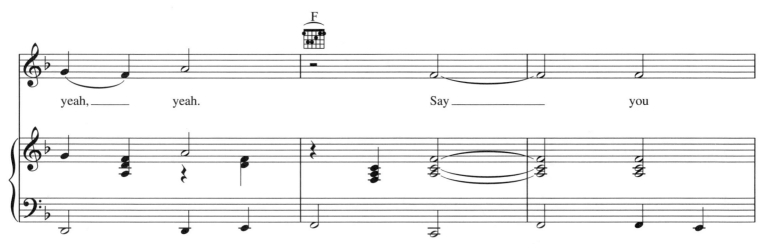

yeah, _____ yeah. Say _____ you

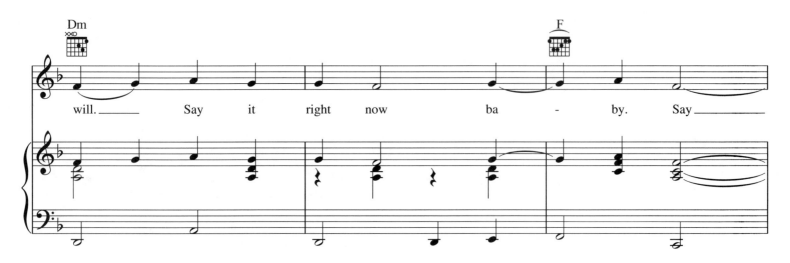

will._____ Say it right now ba - by. Say _____

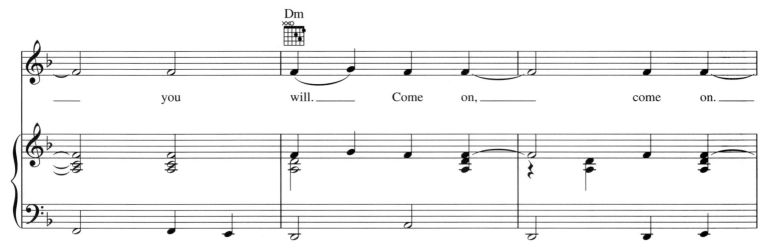

_____ you will._____ Come on,_____ come on._____

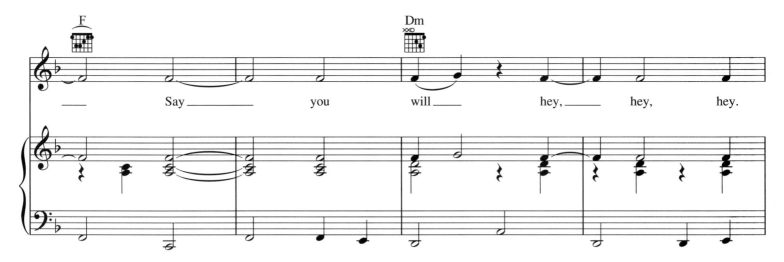

_____ Say_____ you will_____ hey,_____ hey, hey.

_____ Say_____ you will._____ Come on_____ now._____

228

(Say) Say that you love me. (Say) Say that you
(Say) Say that you want me. (Say) You wan - na

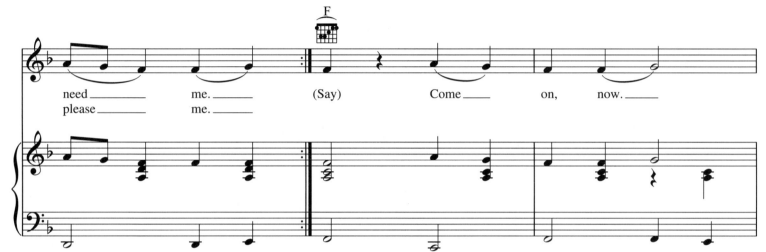

need _____ me. _____ (Say) Come _____ on, now. _____
please _____ me. _____

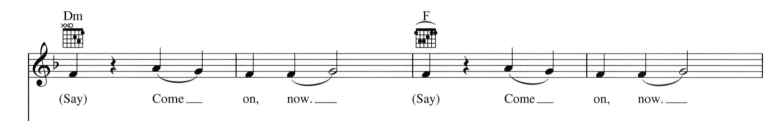

(Say) Come _____ on, now. _____ (Say) Come _____ on, now. ____

(Say.) I still re - mem - ber (Shoo - by

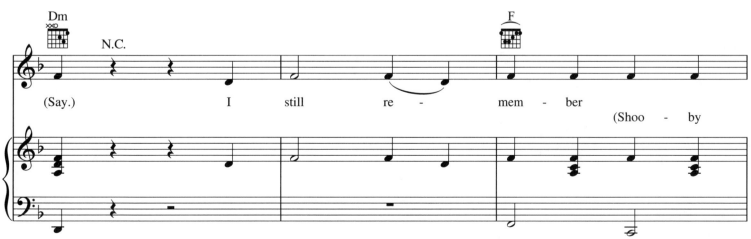

when you used to be nine years old ____

doo - wop.)

(Shoo - by - doo.) yeah, ____ yeah. ____

I was a fool ____ for you from the

bot - tom of my soul, ____ yeah.

Now _____ that you've grown _____ up

you're old e-nough to know, _____

yeah, _____ yeah. _____ You wan-na leave _____

_____ me. You wan-na
(Shoo - by doo - wop.)

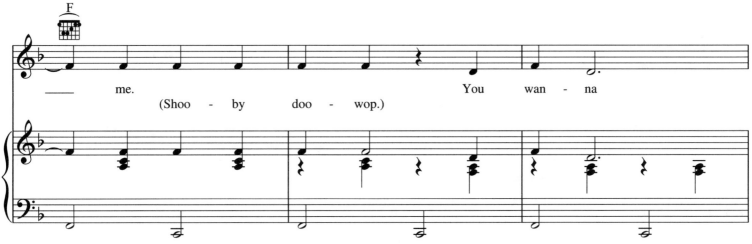

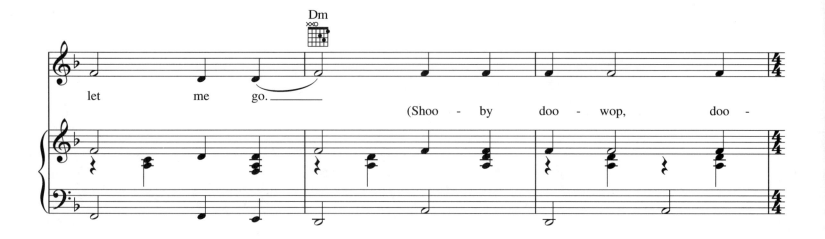

let me go. _____ (Shoo - by doo - wop, doo -

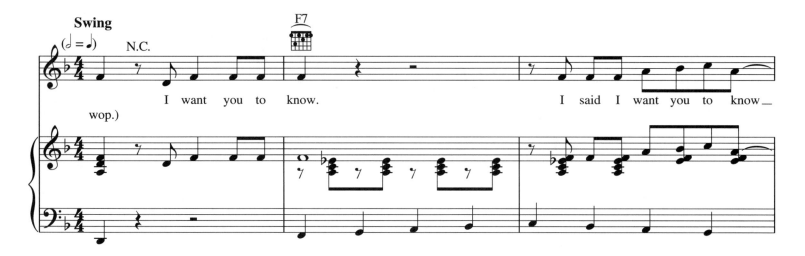

wop.) I want you to know. I said I want you to know _____

_____ right now, yeah. You've been good _____ to me ba - by, _____

bet - ter than I've been to my - self, yeah, hey. And if you ev - er

leave _____ me ___ I don't want no - bod - y else, hey, hey.

I said I want you to know, _____ hey. I said I want you to know ___

Original Tempo

($\downarrow = \downarrow$)

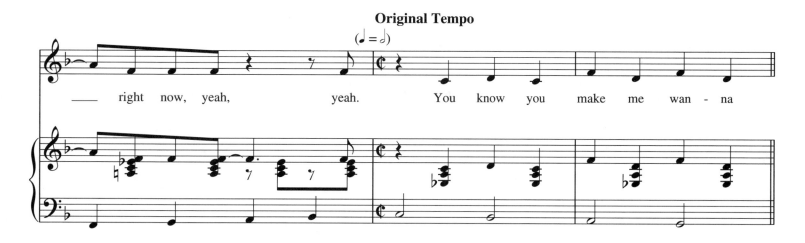

___ right now, yeah, yeah. You know you make me wan - na

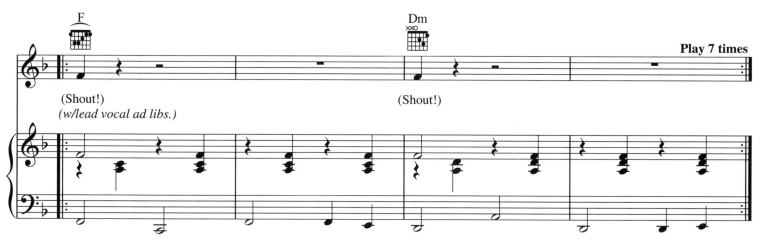

(Shout!)
(w/lead vocal ad libs.)

(Shout!)

Play 7 times

F

Dm

233

(Shout!)   Now   wait_____   a   min - ute.____   I feel

all_____   right._____
(Yeah,   yeah,   yeah,   yeah,   yeah,

Now that I've got my wom - an, I feel   all_____
yeah.)

right.__
     (Yeah, yeah, yeah, yeah, yeah.)   Ev - 'ry time I think a - bout you.   You been so good   to me.

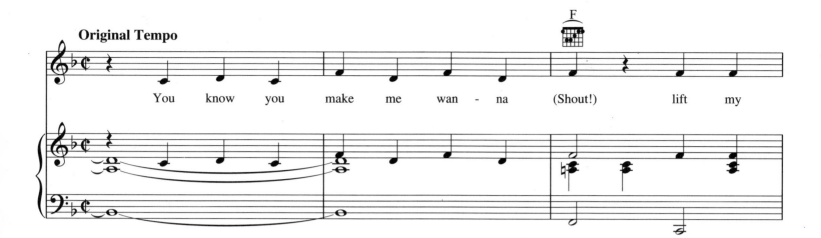

Original Tempo

You know you make me wan - na (Shout!) lift my

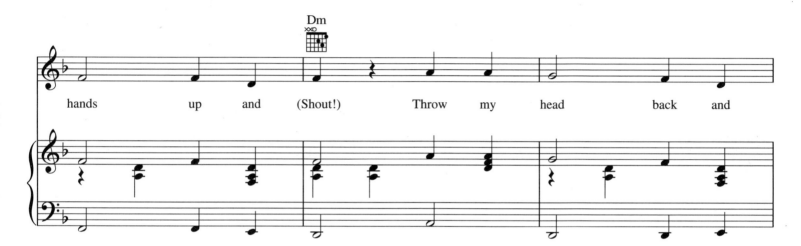

hands up and (Shout!) Throw my head back and

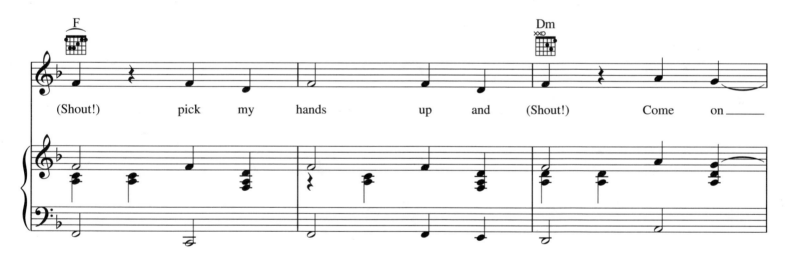

(Shout!) pick my hands up and (Shout!) Come on ___

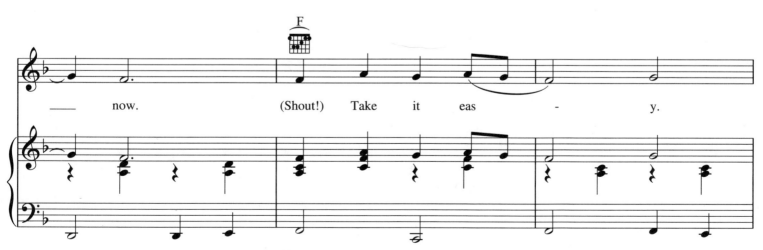

___ now. (Shout!) Take it eas - y.

(Shout!) Take it eas - y. (Shout!) Take it eas -

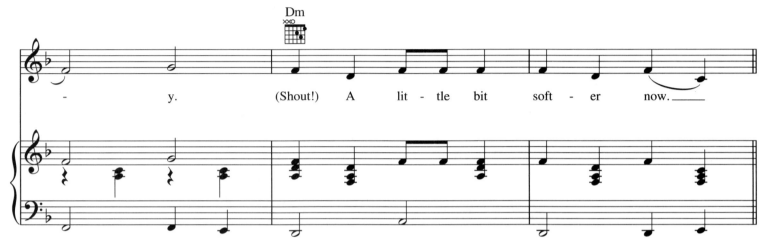

- y. (Shout!) A lit - tle bit soft - er now.___

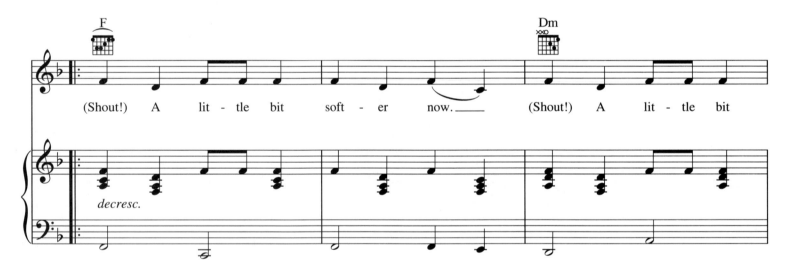

(Shout!) A lit - tle bit soft - er now.___ (Shout!) A lit - tle bit

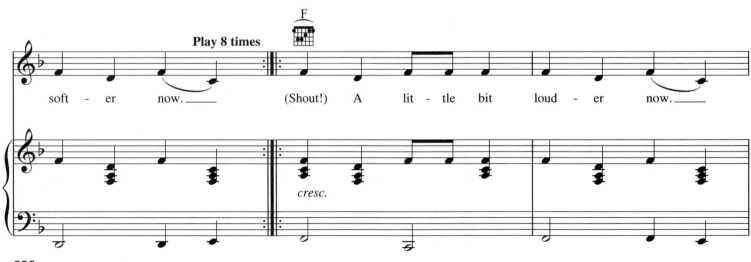

soft - er now.___ (Shout!) A lit - tle bit loud - er now.___

(Shout!) A lit - tle bit loud - er now. _____ (Shout!) Hey, _____

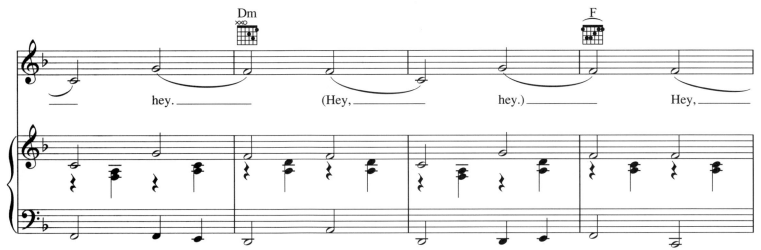

hey. _____ (Hey, _____ hey.) _____ Hey, _____

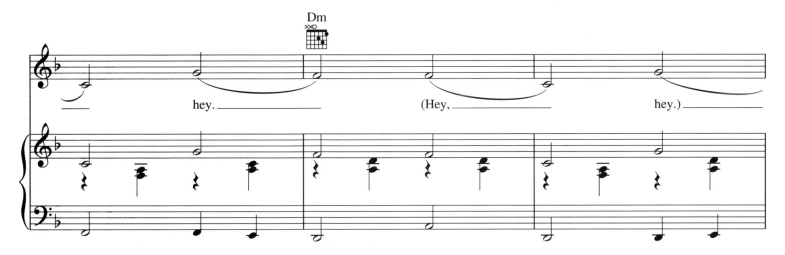

hey. _____ (Hey, _____ hey.) _____

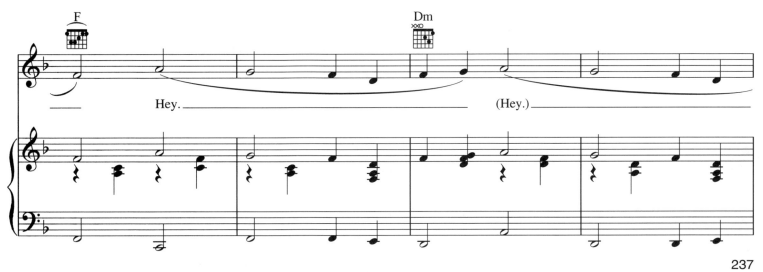

Hey. _____ (Hey.) _____

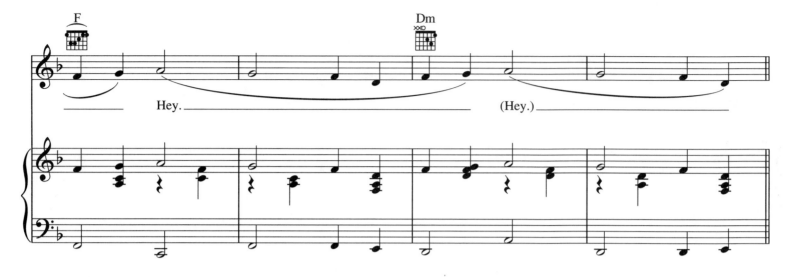

Hey. (Hey.)

Shout now. Jump up and shout now.

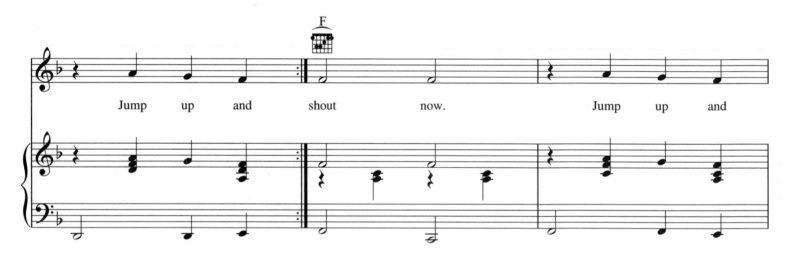

Jump up and shout now. Jump up and

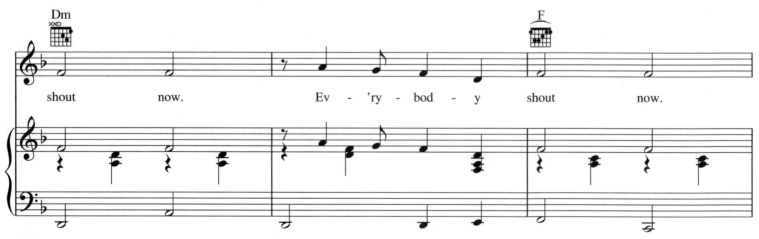

shout now. Ev - 'ry - bod - y shout now.

So You Want to Be a Rock and Roll Star

Words and Music by
Roger McGuinn and Chris Hillman

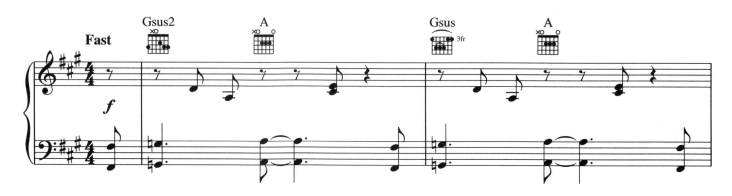

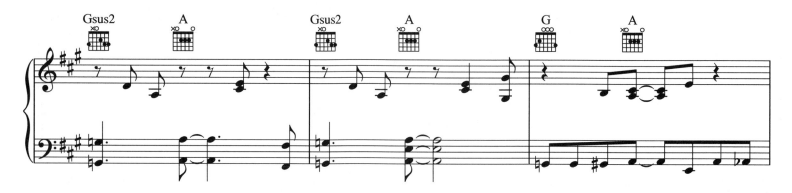

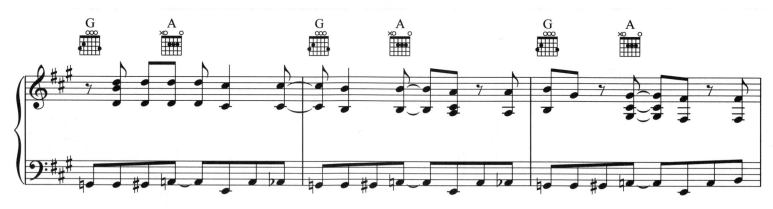

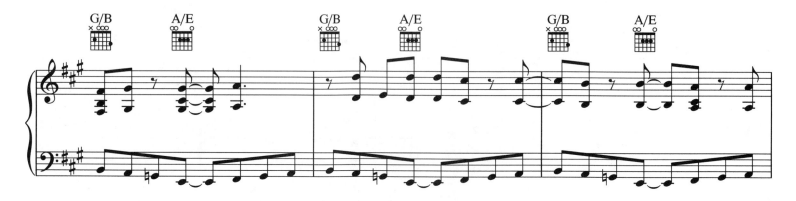

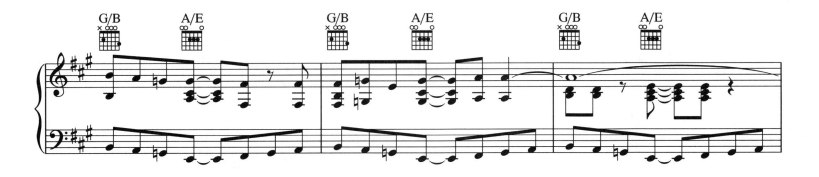

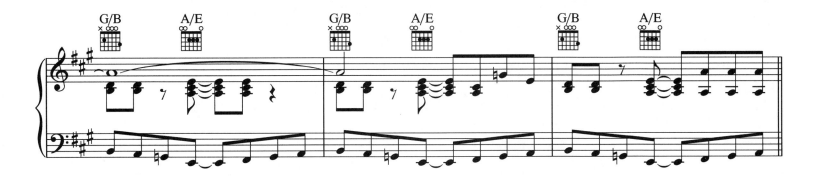

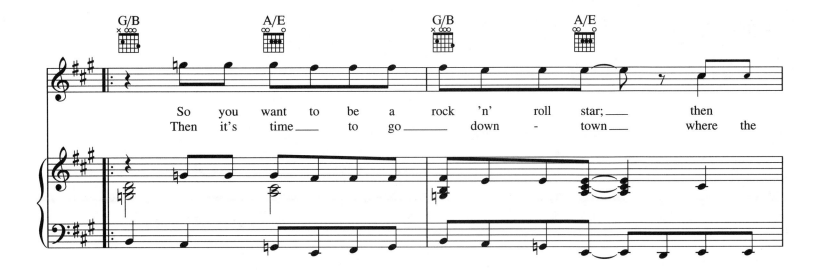

So you want to be a rock 'n' roll star; ____ then
Then it's time ____ to go ____ down - town ____ where the

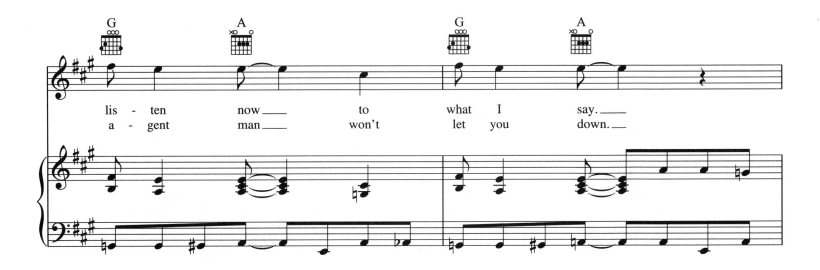

lis - ten now ____ to what I say. ____
a - gent man ____ won't let you down. ____

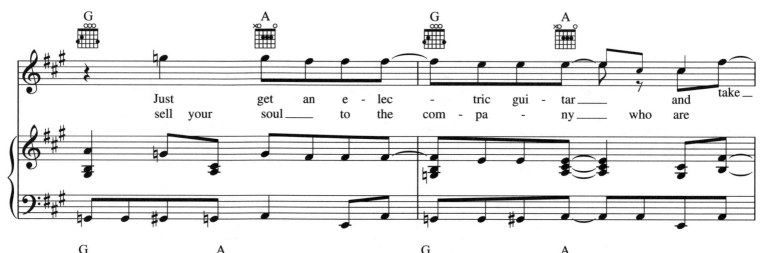

Just get an e - lec - tric gui - tar ___ and take ___
sell your soul ___ to the com - pa - ny ___ who are

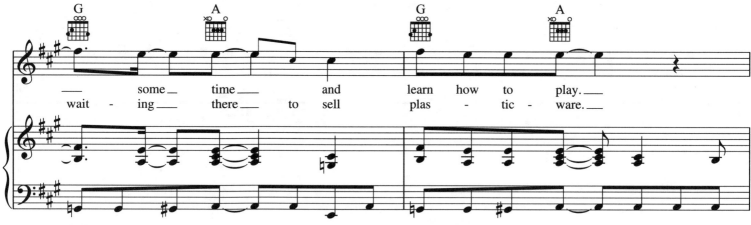

___ some ___ time ___ and learn how to play. ___
wait - ing ___ there ___ to sell plas - tic - ware. ___

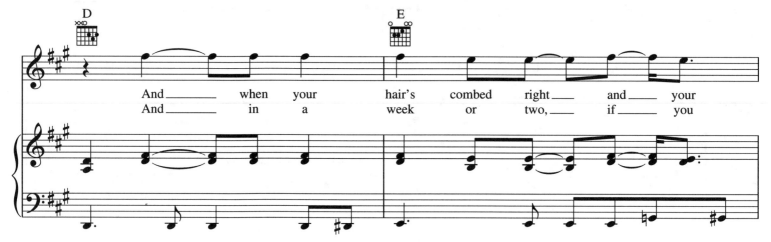

And ___ when your hair's combed right ___ and ___ your
And ___ in a week or two, ___ if ___ you

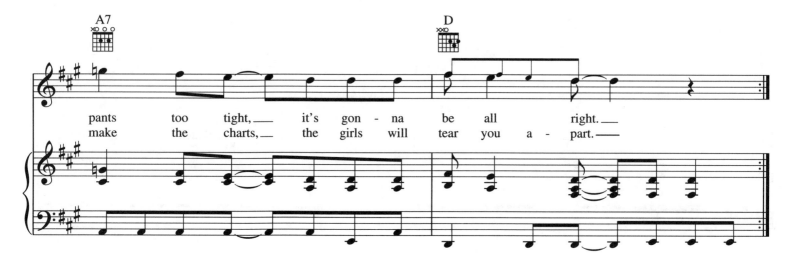

pants too tight, ___ it's gon - na be all right. ___
make the charts, ___ the girls will tear you a - part. ___

242

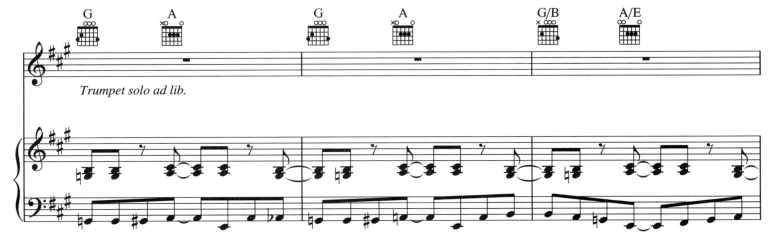

Trumpet solo ad lib.

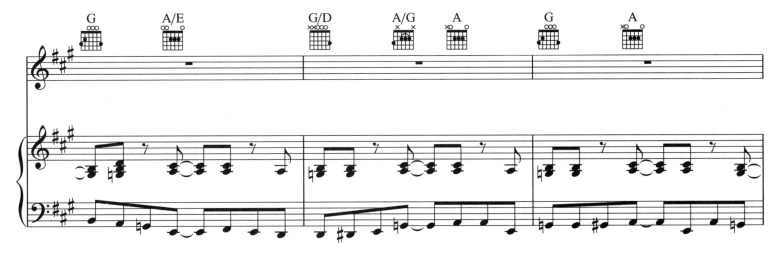

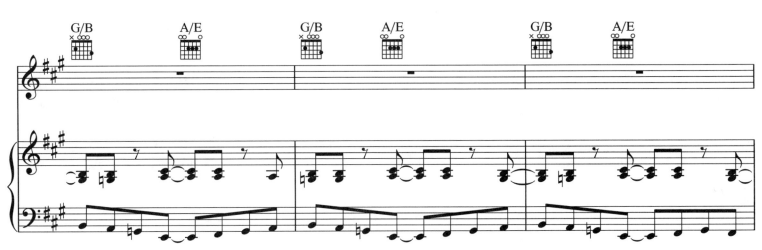

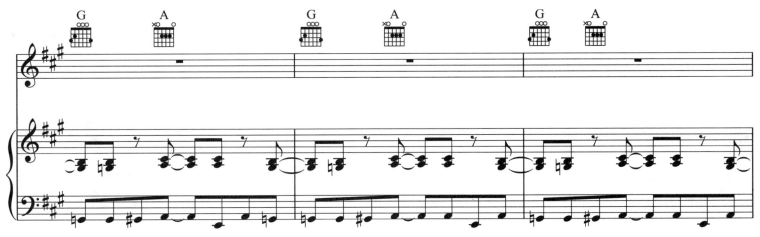

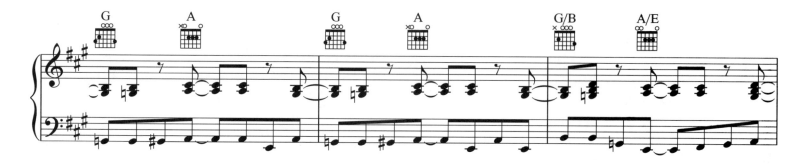

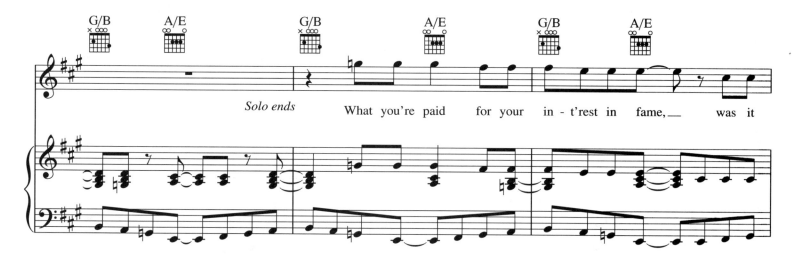

Solo ends

What you're paid for your in - t'rest in fame,___ was it

all a strange game? You're a lit - tle in - sane.___

The mon - ey that came, and the pub - lic ac - claim. Don't for -

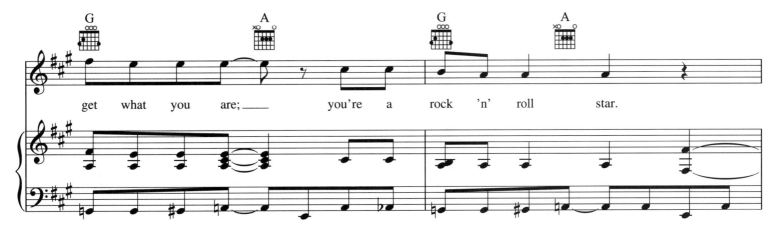

get what you are;___ you're a rock 'n' roll star.

La___ la la la la la___ la la la la la___ la la

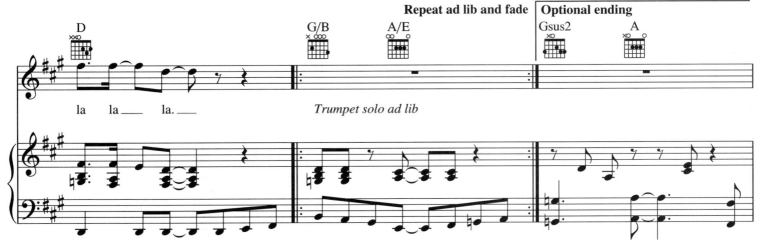

Repeat ad lib and fade | **Optional ending**

la la___ la.___

Trumpet solo ad lib

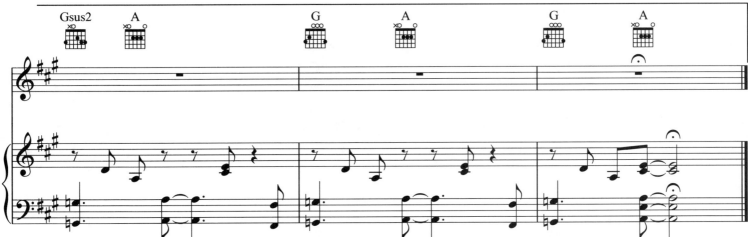

245

Summer in the City

Words and Music by
John Sebastian, Steve Boone
and Mark Sebastian

Moderately, with a steady beat

But at night it's a dif-f'rent world,

Go out and find a girl.___ Come on, come on and dance___ all night,___

de-spite the heat it-'ll be al-right,___ And babe, don't you know it's a pit-y, The

days can't be like the nights, In the sum-mer___ in the cit-y,___ In the

sum - mer____ in the cit - y.____   sum - mer____ in the cit - y.____

(Instrumental)

D.S. and Fade
(Instrumental)

248

Teach Your Children

Words and Music by
Graham Nash

You ... who are on the road ___

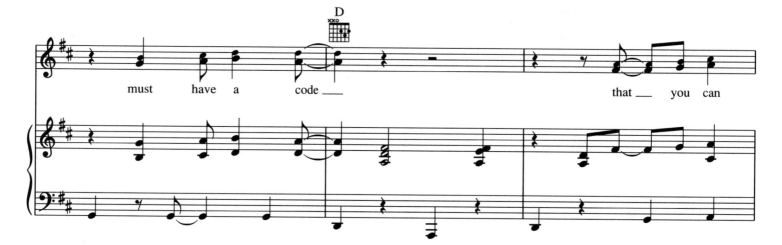

must have a code ___   that ___ you can

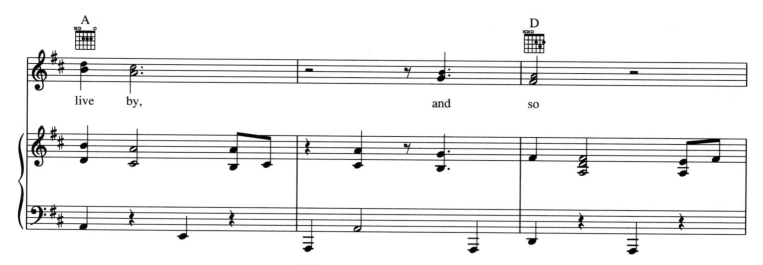

live by,   and   so

be - come ___ your - self,   be - cause ___ the past ___

is   just   a   good - bye.

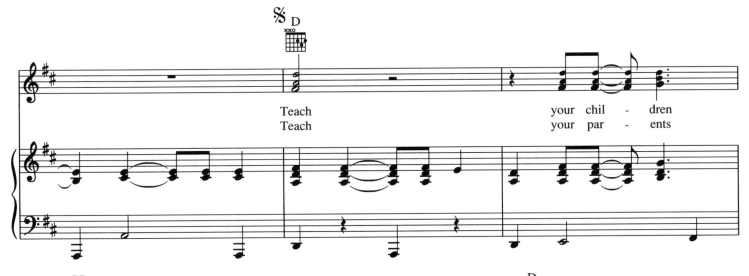

Teach   your chil - dren
Teach   your par - ents

well;   their fa - ther's   hell
well;   their chil - dren's hell

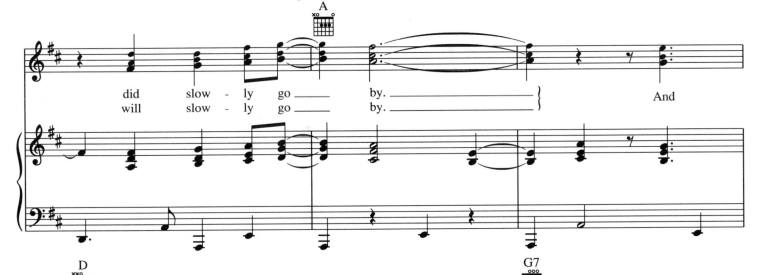

did slow - ly go ____ by. _____   And
will slow - ly go ____ by. _____

feed   then on ____ your   dreams,

the one — they picks, the one — you'll know —

— by. _____ Don't you ev -

- er ask — them why; if they told you, you — would

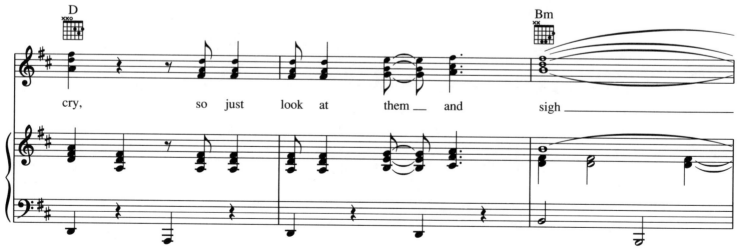

cry, so just look at them — and sigh _____

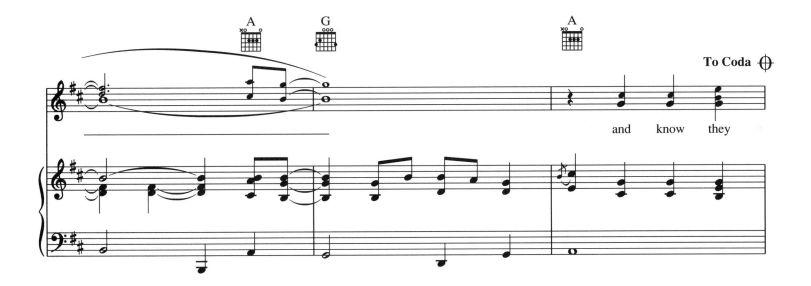

To Coda ⊕

and know they

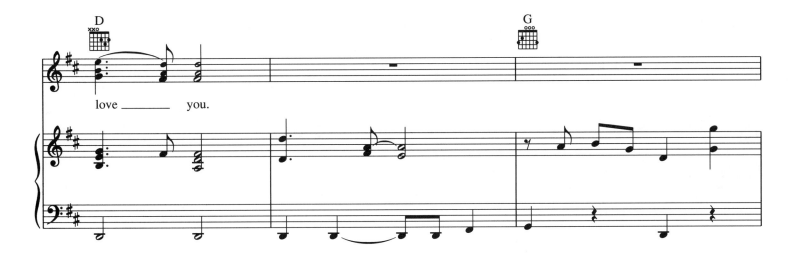

love _____ you.

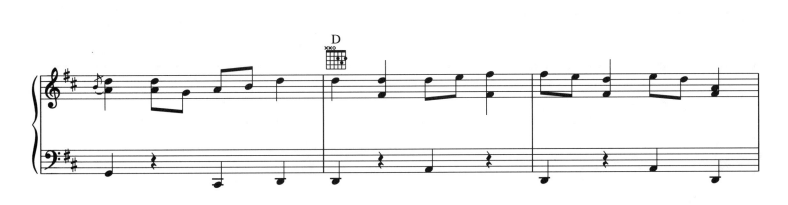

(Can you

And you

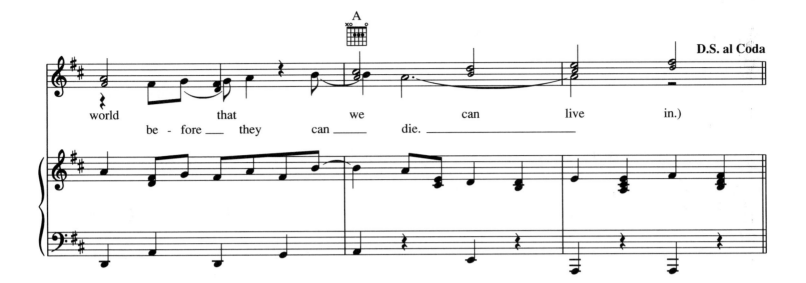

world that we can live in.)
be - fore __ they can __ die. _____

CODA

love _____ you.

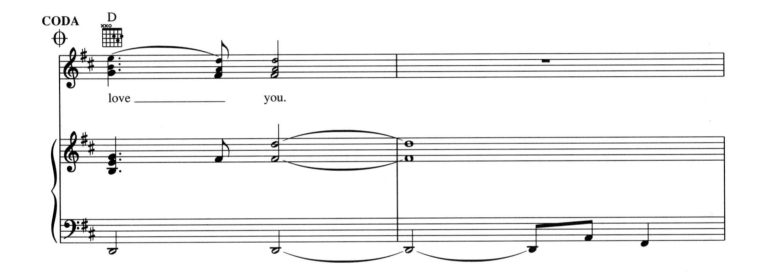

Superstar

Words and Music by
Leon Russell and Bonnie Sheridan

Chorus

ra-di-o.
sad gui-tar. Don't you re-mem-ber you told me you love me, ba-

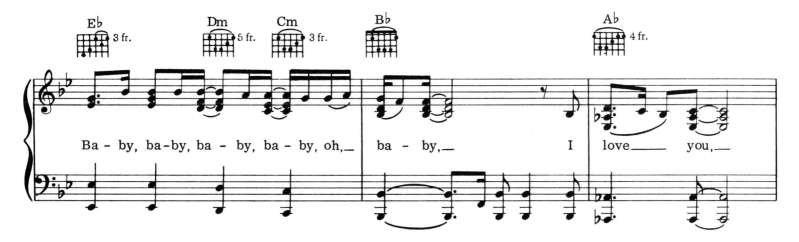

-by? You said you'd be com-ing back this way a-gain may-be.

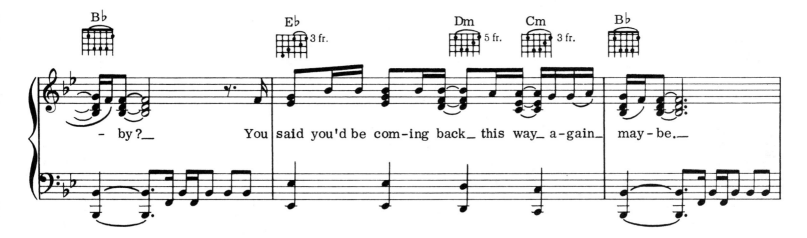

Ba-by, ba-by, ba-by, ba-by, oh, ba-by, I love you,

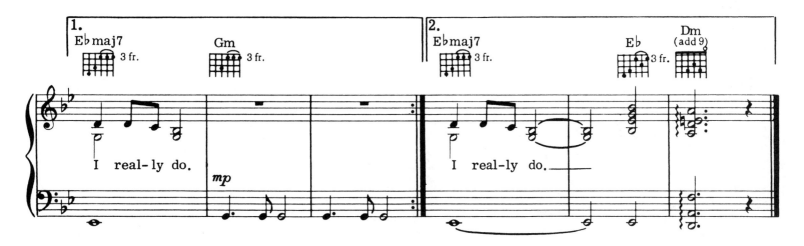

1.
I real-ly do. *mp*

2.
I real-ly do.

Tears in Heaven

Words and Music by
Eric Clapton and Will Jennings

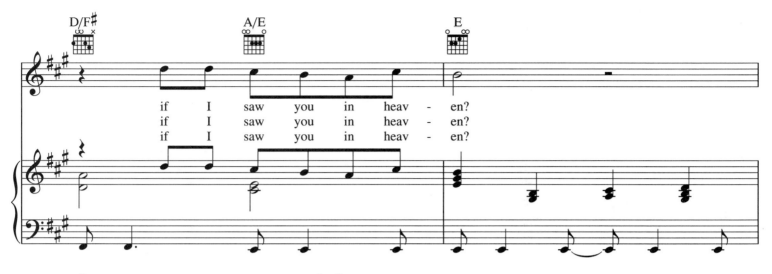

if I saw you in heav - en?
if I saw you in heav - en?
if I saw you in heav - en?

(1.,3.) I must be strong_____ and car - ry on_____
(2.) I'll find my way_____ through night and day_____

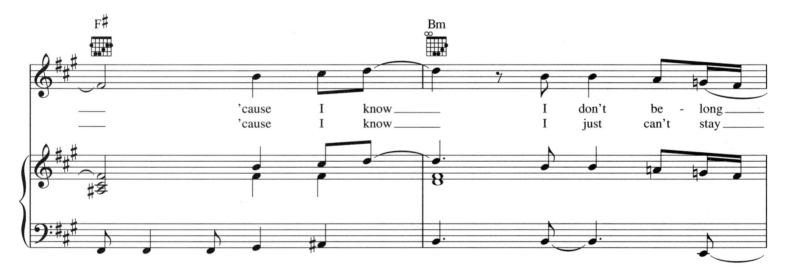

_____ 'cause I know_____ I don't be - long_____
_____ 'cause I know_____ I just can't stay_____

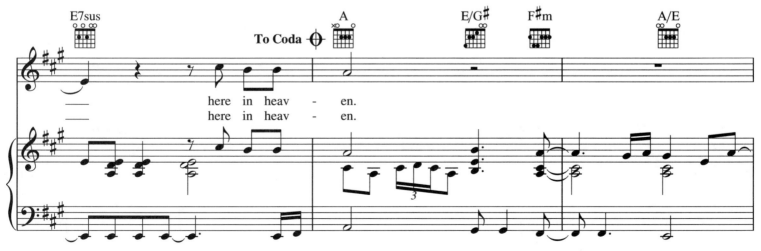

To Coda

_____ here in heav - en.
_____ here in heav - en.

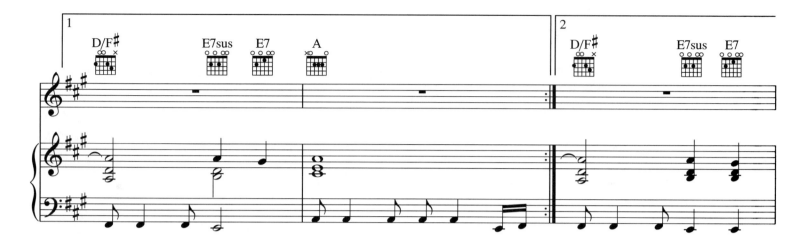

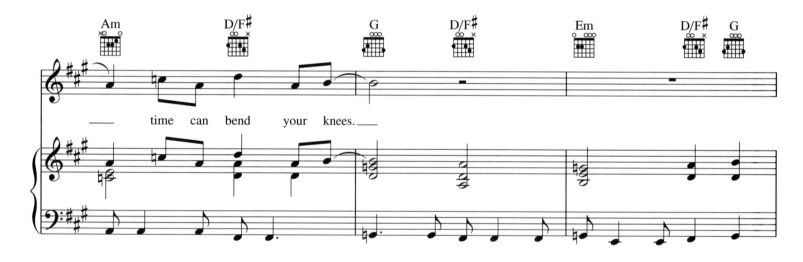

Time can bring you down,

time can bend your knees.

Time can break the heart, have you beg - gin' please, beg - gin' please.

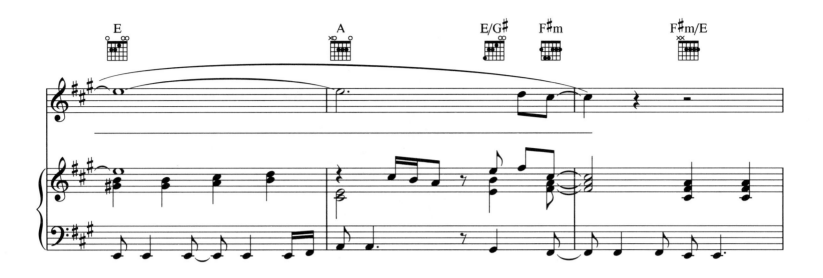

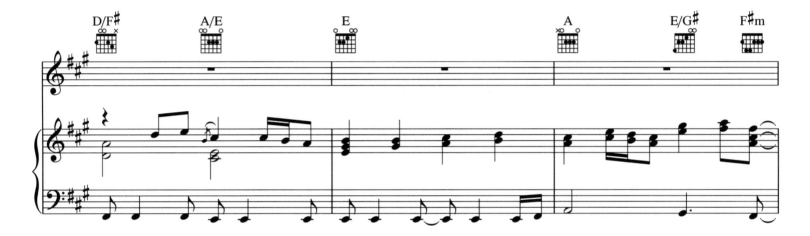

Be - yond the door_____ there's peace, I'm sure,_____

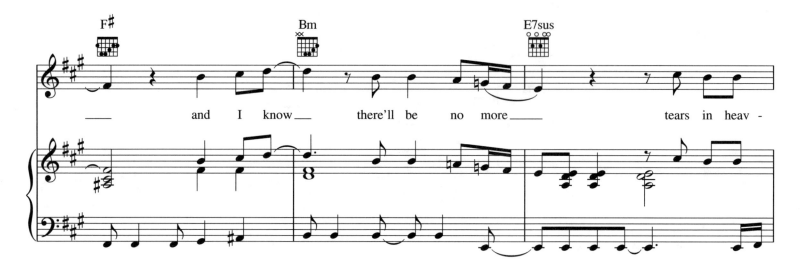

and I know ___ there'll be no more ___ tears in heav-

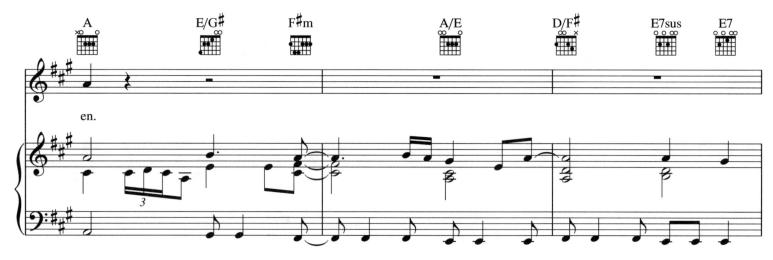

en.

D.S. al Coda

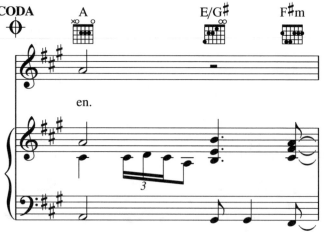

CODA

en.

rall.

Top of the World

Words and Music by
John Bettis and Richard Carpenter

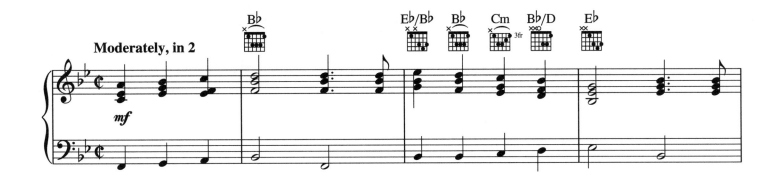

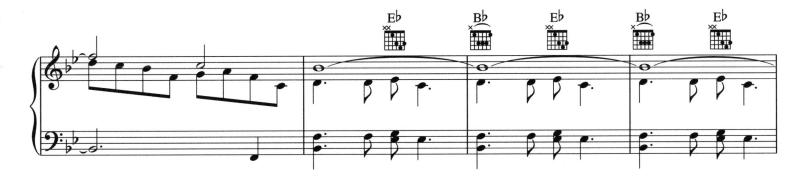

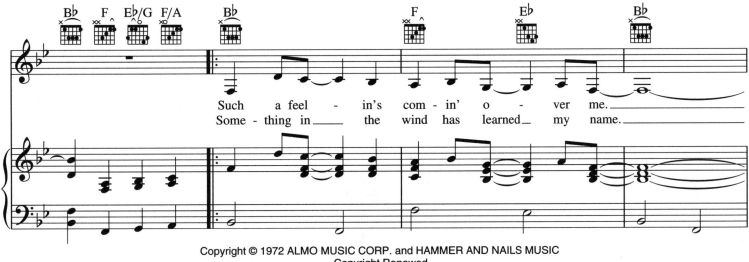

Such a feel - in's com-in' o - ver me.____
Some - thing in____ the wind has learned__ my name.____

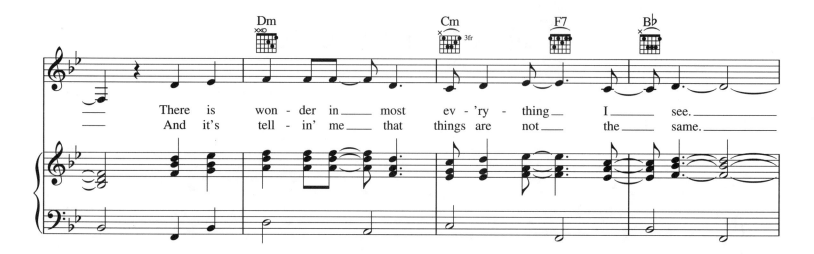

There is won-der in ___ most ev-'ry-thing ___ I ___ see. ___
And it's tell-in' me ___ that things are not ___ the ___ same. ___

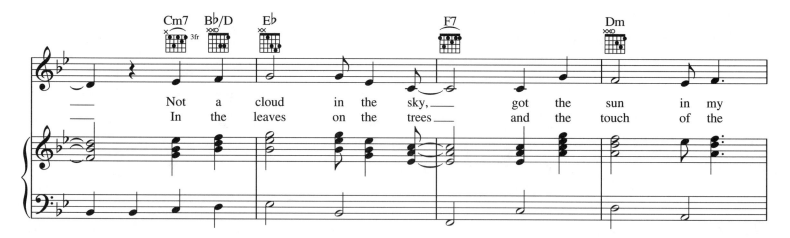

Not a cloud in the sky, ___ got the sun in my
In the leaves on the trees ___ and the sun touch of the

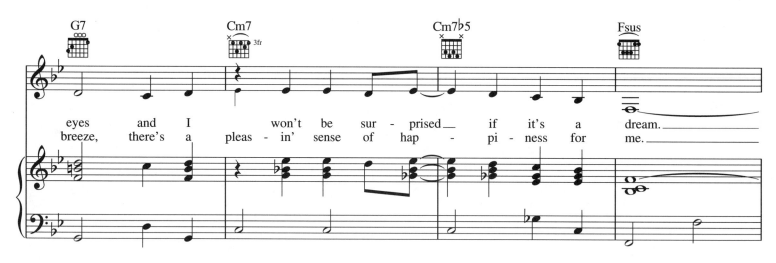

eyes and I won't be sur-prised ___ if it's a dream. ___
breeze, there's a pleas-in' sense of hap-pi-ness for me. ___

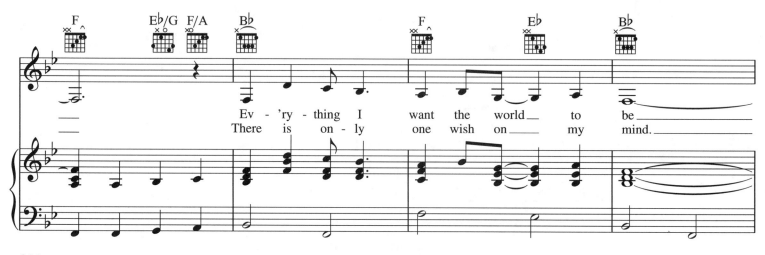

Ev-'ry-thing I want the world ___ to be ___
There is on-ly one wish on ___ my mind. ___

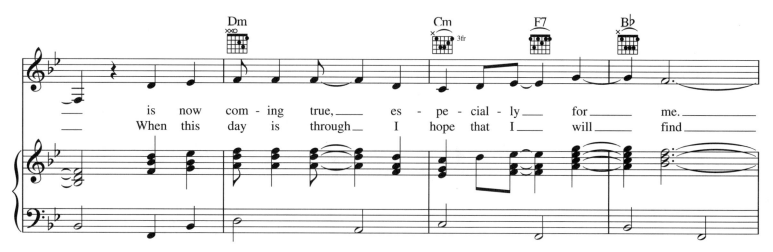

is now com-ing true,___ es - pe - cial-ly ___ for ___ me.___
When this day is through ___ I hope that I ___ will ___ find ___

___ And the rea - son is clear; it's be - cause you are
___ that to - mor - row will be just the same for you and

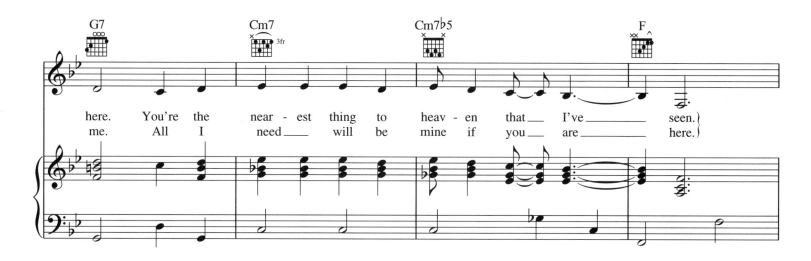

here. You're the near - est thing to heav - en that ___ I've ___ seen.)
me. All I need ___ will be mine if you ___ are ___ here.)

I'm on the top of the world, _____ look - in' down on cre - a -

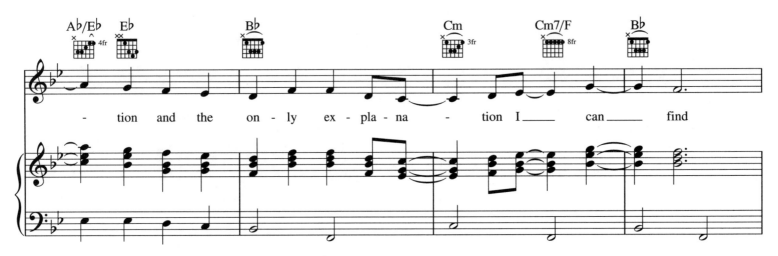

-tion and the on-ly ex-pla-na - tion I ____ can ____ find

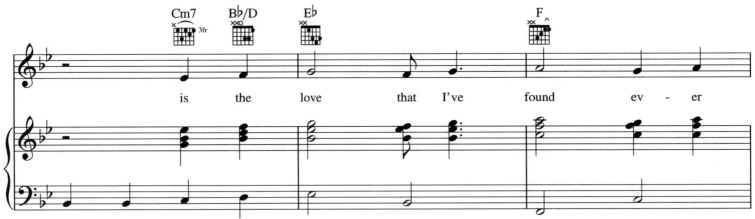

is the love that I've found ev - er

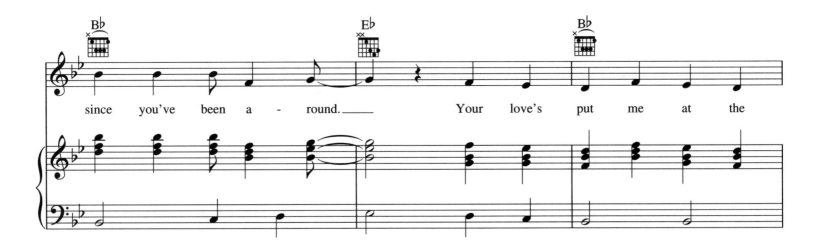

since you've been a - round. ____ Your love's put me at the

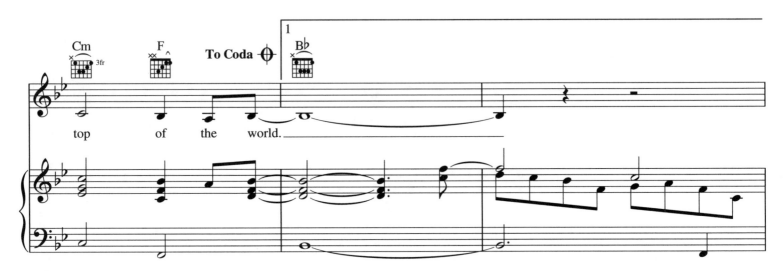

top of the world. ____

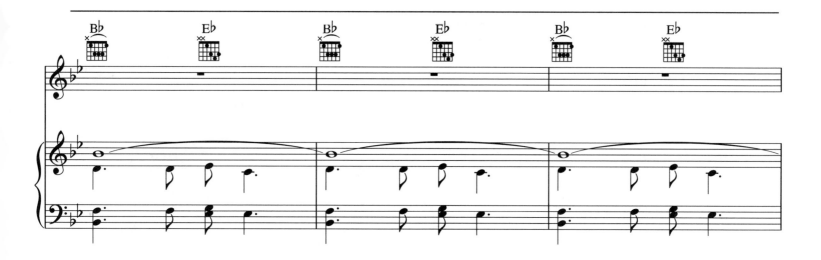

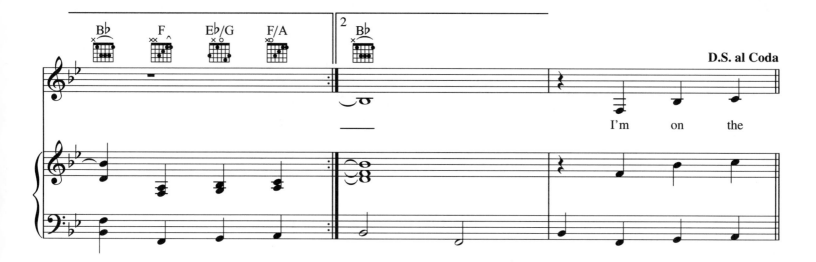

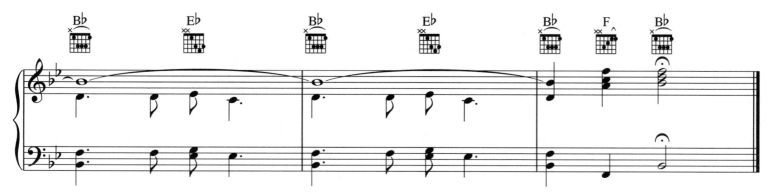

Teen Angel

Words and Music by
Jean Surrey

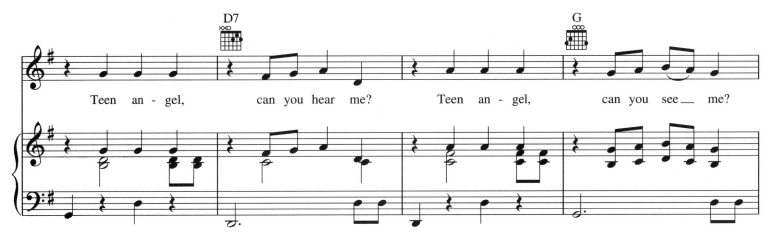

Teen an- gel, can you hear me? Teen an- gel, can you see___ me?

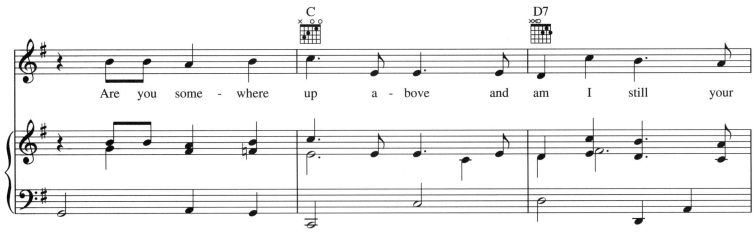

Are you some- where up a- bove and am I still your

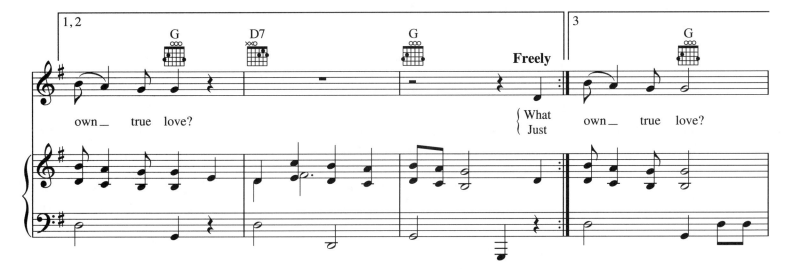

own___ true love? What Just own___ true love?

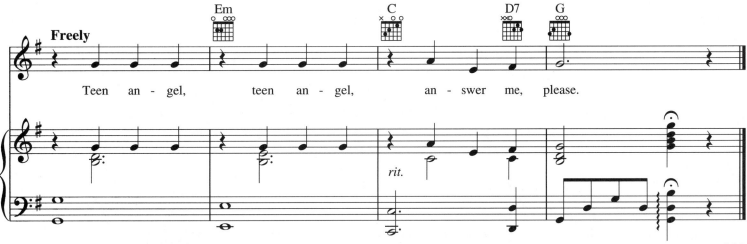

Teen an- gel, teen an- gel, an- swer me, please.

This Masquerade

Words and Music by
Leon Russell

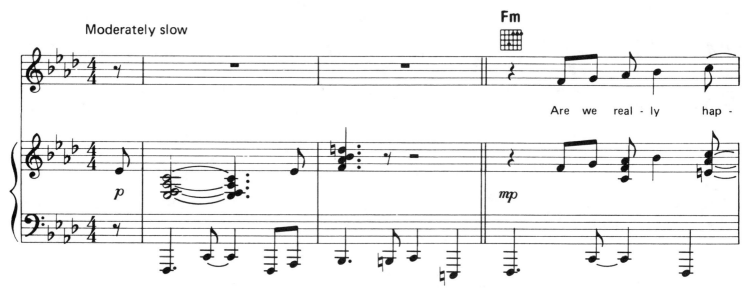

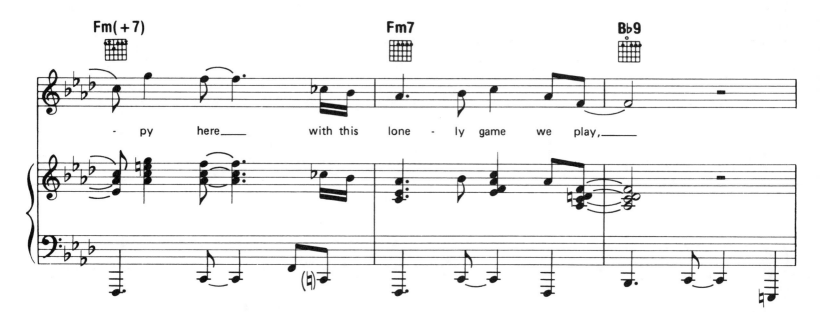

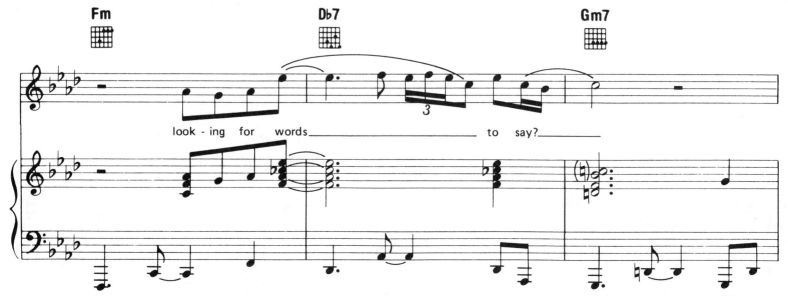

273

*Guitar solo sounds 8va
lower than written.
274

quer - ade._____

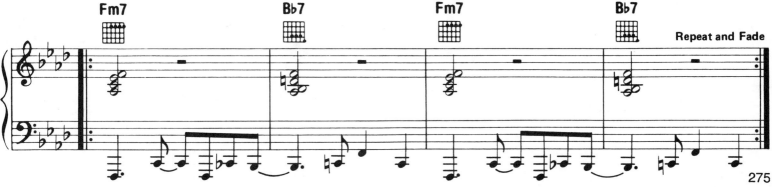

Time in a Bottle

Words and Music by
Jim Croce

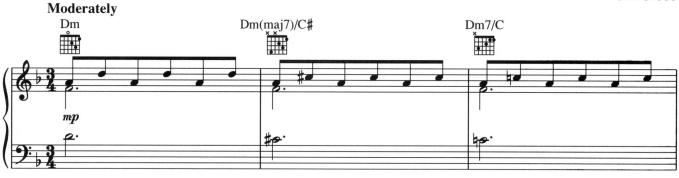

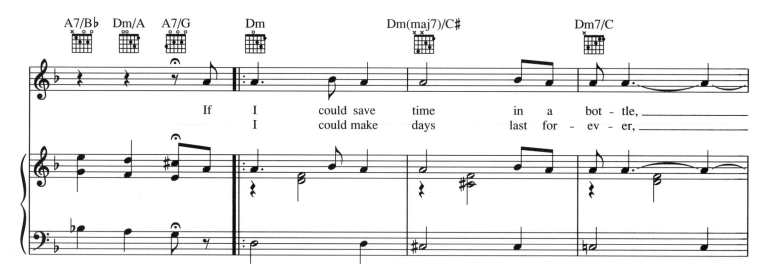

If I could save time in a bot-tle, _____

I could make days last for-ev-er, _____

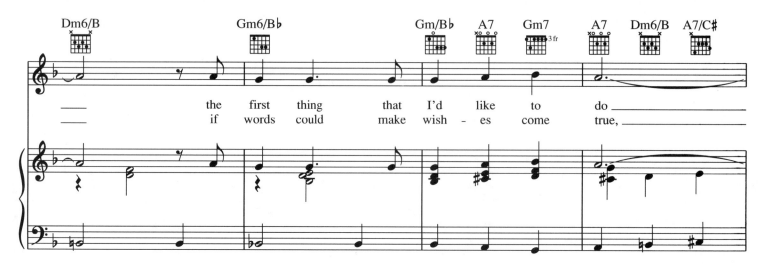

____ the first thing that I'd like to do _____

____ if words could make wish - es come true, _____

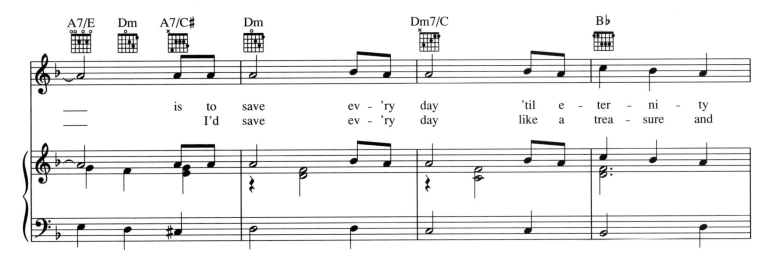

is to save ev-'ry day 'til e-ter-ni-ty
I'd save ev-'ry day like a trea-sure and

pass-es a-way just to spend them with you.
then a-gain I would spend them with you.

If ___ But there nev-er seems to

be e-nough time to do the things you want to do once you

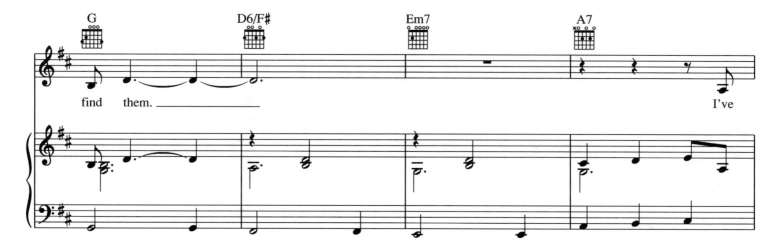

find them. _____ I've

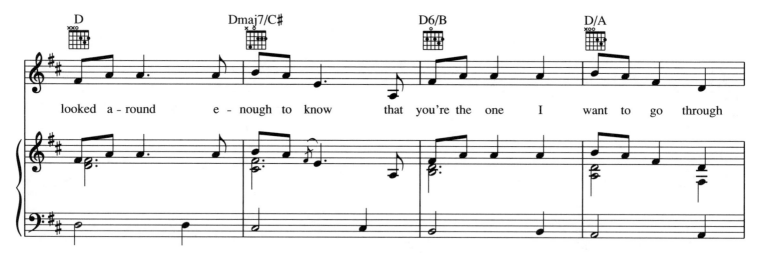

looked a-round e-nough to know that you're the one I want to go through

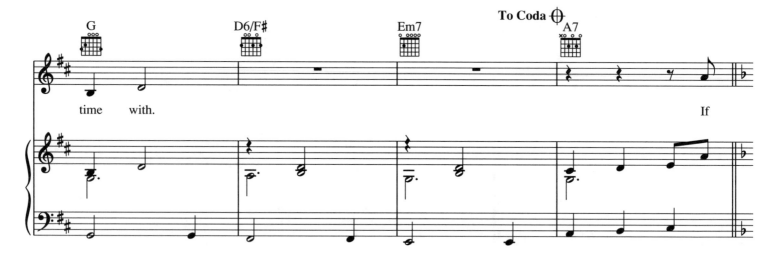

time with. If

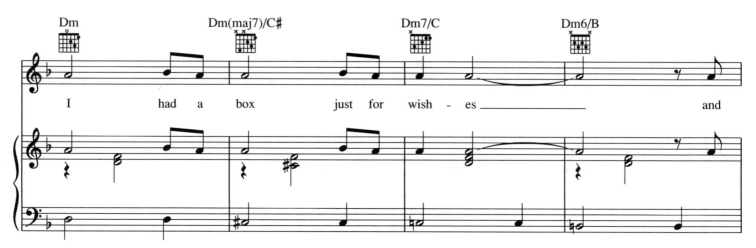

I had a box just for wish-es _____ and

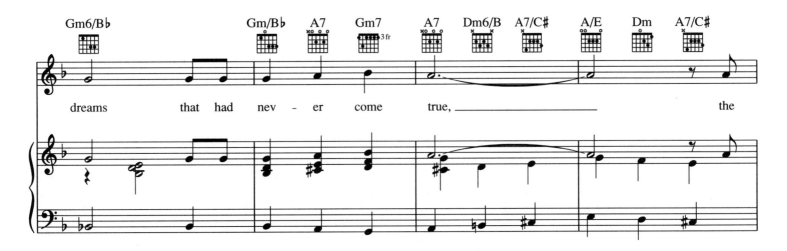

dreams   that had   nev - er   come   true, _____   the

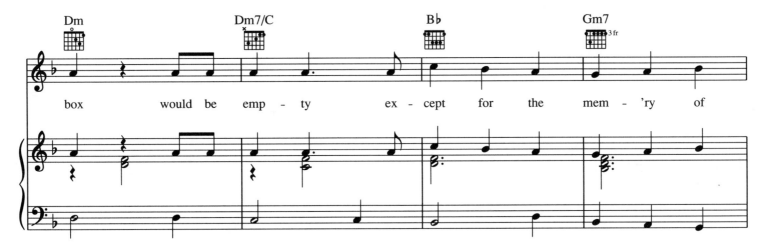

box   would be   emp - ty   ex - cept   for   the   mem - 'ry   of

how   they were   an - swered   by   you. _____   But   there

D.S. al Coda

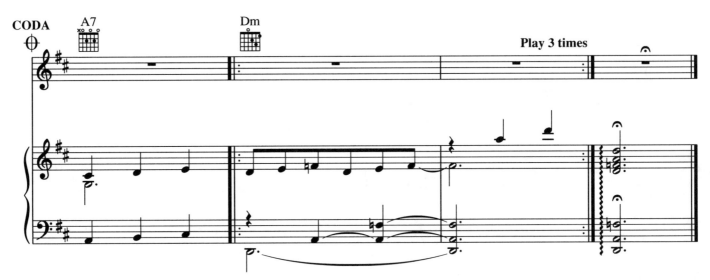

Play 3 times

Travelin' Man

Words and Music by
Jerry Fuller

Easy Rock

I'm a trav-el-in' man and I've made a lot o' stops _____

_____ all o-ver the world; ____ and in ev-er-y port _____ I _____

own the heart __ of at least one love-ly girl. ____ I've a

pret - ty se - ño - ri - ta   wait - in' for me___   down in old Mex - i - co;___

Guitar solo

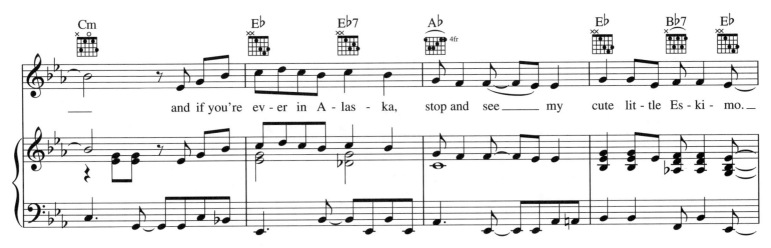

___ and if you're ev - er in A - las - ka, stop and see___ my cute lit - tle Es - ki - mo.___

___ Solo ends   Oh, my sweet frau - lein___ down in Ber - lin town___   makes my heart start to

yearn;___   and my Chi - na doll___ down in old Hong Kong   waits for my re -

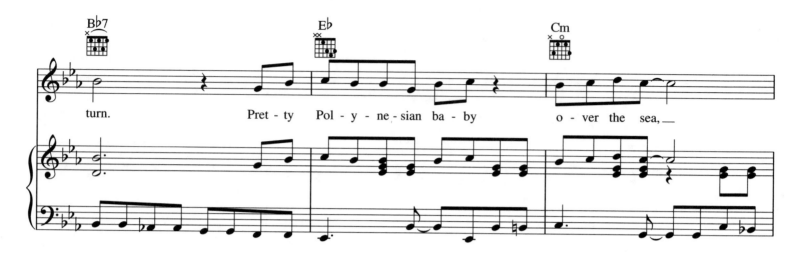

turn. Pret - ty Pol - y - ne - sian ba - by o - ver the sea, ___

I re - mem - ber the night ___ when we walked on the sands of Wai - ki - ki ___ and I

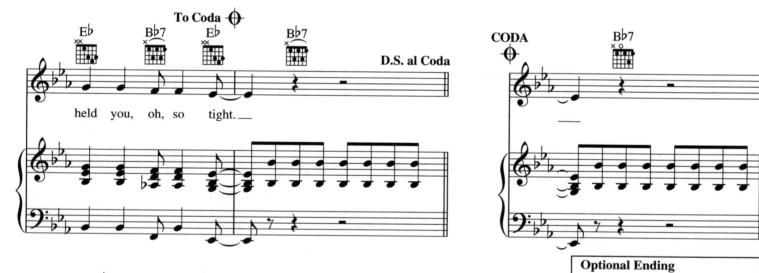

To Coda ⊕

D.S. al Coda

held you, oh, so tight. ___

CODA ⊕

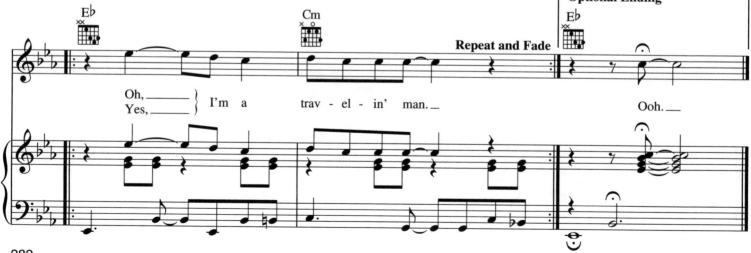

Repeat and Fade

Optional Ending

Oh, ___
Yes, ___ } I'm a trav - el - in' man. ___

Ooh. ___

Yesterday

Words and Music by
John Lennon and Paul McCartney

Moderately, with expression

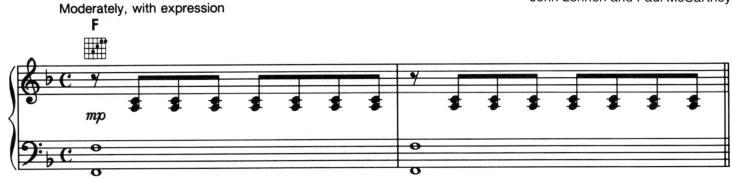

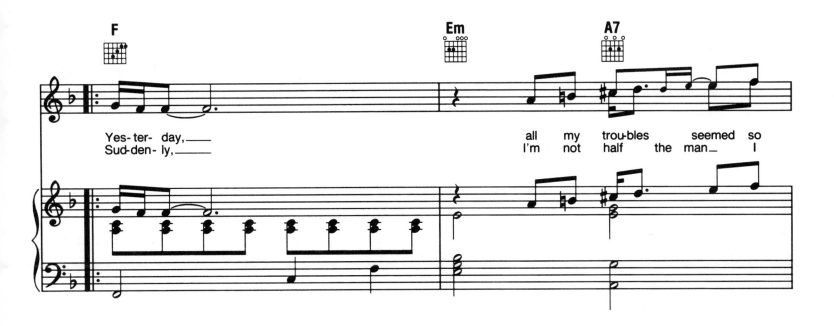

Yes-ter- day,___ all my trou-bles seemed so
Sud-den- ly,___ I'm not half the man___ I

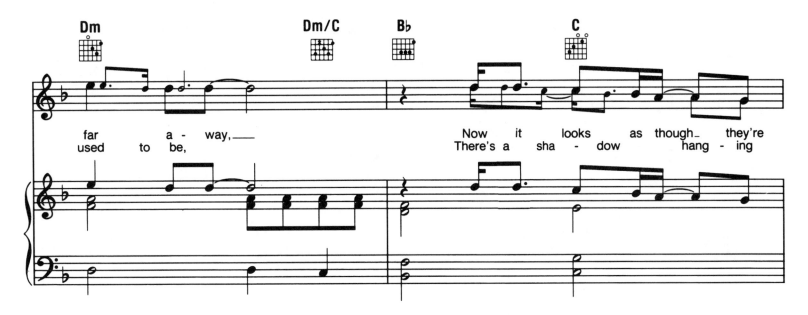

far a- way,___ Now it looks as though___ they're
used to be, There's a sha- dow hang - ing

The Twist

Words and Music by
Hank Ballard

Waiting for a Girl Like You

Words and Music by
Mick Jones and Lou Gramm

You Are So Beautiful

Words and Music by
Billy Preston and Bruce Fisher